Innovative Africa: The new face of Africa

Essays on the rise of Africa's Innovation Age

By Will Mutua & Mbwana Alliy

Edited by Nanjira Sambuli

Innovative Africa: The New Face of Africa:

Essays on the rise of Africa's Innovation Age

Contents

Foreword

'Tech in Africa' has come a long way in a very short time. It took less than five years for a small and fragmented group of pioneers to evolve into a sizeable pan-African community. It includes IT start-up centres, experienced computer literates, profitable start-ups, established businesses serving African and global clients and, most recently, a handful of African hardware companies.

The spread of affordable bandwidth and low-priced hardware have certainly helped this development. But there are less tangible, yet more important, drivers. The possibility to work for and with a global community and at par with that community is a great motivator. So is the prospect of independently earning a living and a reputation where high potential jobs are scarce.

The potential of African IT-driven innovation is immense. The decreasing transaction costs for anything that can be transformed in the shape of bits and bytes, including money, have opened a whole new world of feasible business models and worthwhile initiatives. Some of my own favourite examples are intercontinental co-creation, micro-insurance and new imaging technologies in the health sector. This e-book parades many of such initiatives as examples and case studies.

Unfortunately, the potential for abuse is also immense. The same software that can map conflict hotspots during a crisis can be used to map and target the opposition's supporters or minority groups. The mining of mobile provider's data allows for detailed profiling of individuals, including their political preferences. A first glimpse of this was when Kenya's 2007 - 2008 post-election violence was orchestrated with hate-filled SMS messages. *Technology does not change a society. It exacerbates and accelerates trends prevailing in a society.*

To strengthen the positive potential and prevent the harm, we need keen observers of the technology space. We need observers who are able to take one step back from the hype of the month, who are able to set us thinking by posing the underlying questions and provoking us with their reflections. Right from the beginning, Will and Mbwana have been close observers of this space. *Afrinnovator.com* has been a valuable source of inspiration for those seeking to develop and thrive with the positive potential of African innovation.

This book is a timely contribution to the emerging discourse on how Africa's next generation wants to use and shape technology for society. It debates the merits of different strategies to further grow the industry from the individual choice to become a tech entrepreneur, to the multi-million dollar IT campuses and cities. It goes further to question some of the current industry beliefs. Enjoy the read and join the debate.

Dr. Jasper Grosskurth

Jasper is the Director of Research & Strategy at Research Solutions Africa and author of 'Futures of Technology in Africa'.

Preface

Africa is Rising!

After decades of being considered the 'dark continent', Africa today enjoys a time of renewed hope and excitement. In the past, the so-called *four horsemen of Africa's apocalypse* – famine, disease, war and corruption – have dominated the global perception of Africa and perhaps rightfully so. However, a new age has dawned on the continent. This is no longer the hopeless continent but a very hopeful one indeed. The continent's recent economic growth has been quite amazing with several countries growing at record levels, and the continent as a whole showing consistent economic performance that is projected to continue into the rest of the decade. Africa has also shown great resilience to global economic crises. Her best performing economies have been labeled the *Lion Economies*, and the pace of their growth has surpassed that of the so-called *Asian Tiger Economies* in recent times.

Technology and Innovation are playing a big part in shaping Africa's future and will continue to do so. This collection of essays on the '*New face of Africa*' posits an

African continent where technology, innovation and entrepreneurship create new opportunities for even further growth on the continent. The uptake and growth of mobile telephony on the continent, for instance, has been indicative of this. The continent has been a leader in innovations such as mobile money with innovation hubs springing up across the continent facilitating a generation of young tech entrepreneurs. Governments are also making significant investments in ICT development, but much more can and should be done.

We look at a wide array of issues that affect the creation, growth and sustainability of startup and innovation ecosystems around the continent. The book does not seek to address issues at the level of a specific country or locality, but instead looks at things from a broad and high level, with the intention of highlighting issues that are pertinent across borders and cultures. Indeed, some aspects may apply more within some country or culture than others ("*Africa is not a country*").

The book is divided into two parts: The first, "*Investigating Technology Innovation and Entrepreneurship in Africa*", takes a look at the current state of things and makes observations of what progress has been made, existing challenges and opportunities as well as providing specific recommendations that startups, investors and government can use to further technology innovation and entrepreneurship on the continent.

The second part *"In Search of a Model for Technology Innovation and Entrepreneurship Ecosystems that fits the African Context"* takes a close up view of three innovative economies: Silicon Valley, China and Israel, from which we try to glean a few lessons about startup ecosystems that could be applied within the African context in order to come up with a (perhaps hybrid) model that works best for the continent and specific nations within the continent.

Will Mutua, Founder Afrinnovator

Part 1: Investigating Technology Innovation and Entrepreneurship in Africa

Innovative Africa: The New Face of Africa

By Will Mutua

World renowned artist Shakira proclaimed "It's time for Africa!" and millions around the globe echoed her words as they sang to the infectious tune of the official 2010 FIFA World Cup song, the world's largest soccer event having found a venue in Africa for the first time. It is a new era for Africa. The world is increasingly shifting its mentality about the continent, and the continent is becoming more and more confident of her place in today's globalized world. Perhaps the poster child of this paradigm shift in how the world perceives Africa is the case of two articles published on one of the most authoritative magazines in the world, *The Economist*. At the turn of the millennium, The Economist sported a cover page image that depicted an African soldier wielding a weapon cropped into the shape of the map of Africa and proclaiming "The hopeless continent!" The article proceeded to cite the looming despair in many of the continent's states as a result of the so-called *'Four Horsemen of Africa's Apocalypse'* - corruption, disease, war and poverty.

A decade later, The Economist turned on its heel, now labeling Africa "The hopeful continent", this time sporting a more picturesque image, a child flying a rainbow colored kite in the shape of Africa.

A key contributor to this rise has been the uptake and growth of innovative technology. Today, "Africa", "Technology" and "Innovation" are terms that you will often find in the same sentence. Technology and particularly mobile telephony has radically changed the face of the continent and the lives of her people.

Mobile Africa

The penetration of mobile technology in Africa has been radical and unprecedented. Africa is the fastest growing mobile market in the world and is the second largest, after Asia, although it has been predicted that Africa could outgrow Asia. According to the GSM Association, mobile subscriptions have grown almost 20% each year for the past five years. The GSMA, according to its November 2011 Africa Mobile Observatory report, predicts that there will be over 700 million subscribers by the end of 2012; there were already close to 650 million subscribers in the fourth quarter of 2011, about 65% of the total potential market. In terms of subscriptions, Nigeria leads the pack with over 90 million subscribers.

According to the GSMA report, mobile operators make a direct contribution of 3.0% to Africa's aggregate GDP, with actual contribution at the country level ranging from 0.7% in Sudan and Ethiopia to as high as 6.0% in Senegal.

Mobile has also been a key asset to increasing Internet penetration in Africa. In Kenya, for example, the mobile phone is the primary means by which people access the Internet. According to statistics from the Communications Commission of Kenya, out of a total of 6.15 million Internet subscriptions, mobile data/internet subscriptions account for 6.07 million of those.

It is no wonder that mobile is a key area of innovation in Africa. If you want to reach the widest distribution with your service, you have to have it on mobile.

Mobile Innovation

Innovation in mobile technologies has led to the creation of services that have led to great developments in various sectors such as finance, health and agriculture.

Mobile money, and specifically the success story of MPESA, is a mobile innovation poster child in the financial services sector. Leveraging the wide distribution of mobile phones and basic, ubiquitous mobile technology such as SMS has led to the financial inclusion of millions of Africans who would otherwise be termed as 'unbanked'. In Kenya, there are currently about 19 million mobile money subscriptions, representing about 70% of total mobile subscriptions. In Nigeria, the Central Bank of Nigeria has issued about 16 licenses to mobile money operators with the mobile money market valued at US $25 billion.

Total African mobile money transfers are expected to exceed $200 billion in 2015, approximately 18% of the continent's GDP.

In the agricultural sector, two examples of innovative services stand out. *Esoko* is a fast-growing software company headquartered in Accra, focused on improving agricultural processes through creating software for collecting, analyzing and sharing data related to agriculture. Esoko is an information channel that individuals, agri-businesses, governments and projects use to collect and send out market information using simple text messaging. The company is no w active in multiple countries across the continent including Malawi, Nigeria, Cameroon, Mozambique, Ivory Coast and Burkina Faso.

In Kenya, yet another innovative company founded by four smart ladies, M-FARM is using SMS technology to enable farmers to get current price information, aggregate farmers needs and connect them with farm input suppliers and enable farmers to sell their produce collectively.

There are multiple mHealth initiatives across the continent. Just as an example of the amazing innovation taking place where mobile technology meets health, students at Uganda's Makerere University came up with a mobile app for taking pregnancy scans. The app, called WinSenga, involves connecting the funnel-like Pinard Horn, a listening device, to a smartphone through an external microphone. The app records the sounds from the mother's belly and contains an analysis program that produces reports detailing the position, age, weight, breathing pattern and heart rate of the unborn baby. Combine such an app with the declining cost of smartphones and you have a powerful means of addressing health issues such as maternal deaths.

Africa Online

Just a few years ago, Africa stood more or less as a kind of 'digital island', largely disconnected from the rest of the world via undersea fiber. The continent depended on satellite technology to connect to the Internet, a situation that translated to exorbitantly high Internet costs.

In a few short years the situation is totally reversed; there are almost too many undersea fiber optic cables connecting Africa to the rest of the world. As a result, wholesale prices for Internet bandwidth have decreased by as much as 90% from previous levels based on satellite access, and the cost savings are slowly being trickled down to the retail level. While the continent is connected to the world like never before, the challenge with delivering broadband to the African consumer still remains at the last mile connection. But as we have noted before, the mobile phone has been very instrumental at ensuring even the remotest of users are connected to the web.

Figure 1: 3G coverage across Kenya

The introduction of what could be termed as low-end, low-cost smartphones promises to further increase Internet penetration on the continent. In Kenya, Huawei introduced its $100 Android-powered IDEOS Smartphone in partnership with the country's largest MNO, Safaricom in 2011. The phone sold like hotcakes, rapidly becoming the country's top-selling Smartphone. This year, Samsung unveiled the Samsung Galaxy Pocket another Android-powered low cost Smartphone. It is projected that device manufacturers will increasingly create these low-end, low-cost Smartphones making Internet-powered mobile devices more and more accessible to a wider population.

Africa's international Internet bandwidth has experienced some significant growth in a relatively short period of time, rising from 100 Gbps (Gigabits per second) in 2008, to 500 Gbps in 2010 and expected to hit 1 Tbps (Terabytes per second) in 2012. That's a 10-fold increase in 4 years! According to Africa Bandwidth Maps:

"Africa's international Internet bandwidth will reach the 1 Tbps mark during 2012. By December 2011, Africa's total international Internet bandwidth reached 801 Gbps, a 60% increase compared to 2010. This was split between North Africa, which increased by 45% to reach 433 Gbps, and

Sub-Saharan Africa which increased by 82% to reach 368 Gbps. Africa previously reached the 500 Gbps mark in late 2010, and the 100 Gbps mark during 2008"

Figure 2: Africa undersea cables 2009 illustration by Steve Song – manypossibilities.net/african-undersea-cables/

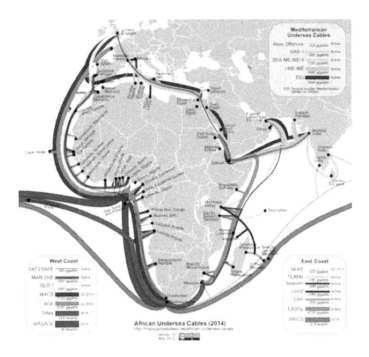

Figure 3: Current and future Africa undersea cables illustration by Steve Song – manypossibilities.net/african-undersea-cables/

While the number of Internet users in Africa represents a mere 6.2% as at December 31st 2011, according to Internet World Stats, Internet penetration has been growing rapidly over the years across the continent. Internet penetration stood at 13.5% of the population, having risen a staggering 2,988.4% since the year 2000, the highest increment globally, seconded by the Middle East which saw a rise of 2,244.8%. At the same time period, Nigeria led, and still leads, on the continent in terms of number of Internet users with 45 million plus users, Egypt, Morocco, Kenya and South Africa followed in that order with 21.7, 15.5, 10.5 and 6.8 million users respectively.

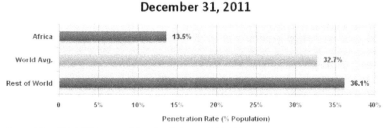

Source Internet World Stats - www.internetworldstats.com/stats1.htm
139,875,242 estimated Internet users in Africa for December 31, 2011
Copyright © 2012, Miniwatts Marketing Group

Figure 4: Internet penetration in Africa

With the efforts of organizations such as Google in Africa, the Internet landscape has seen other dramatic improvements and will continue to do so in the future. Google, for example has deployed its Google Global Cache (GGC) technology in some countries across the continent leading to massive increments in local Internet traffic. For example, Orange Uganda experienced an increment in local traffic from 3Mbps to 30Mbps in just two weeks as a result of partnering with Google to deploy GGC in January of

2011; in neighboring Kenya, local traffic rose 300% from 100Mbps to 400Mbps with the introduction of GGC.

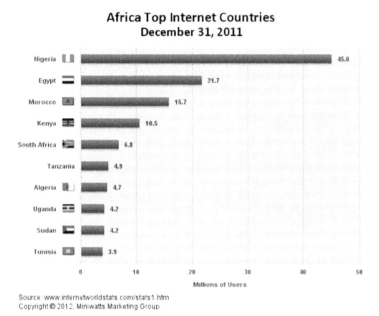

Figure 5: Top Internet countries in Africa 2011

Increased access to the web has led to scores of young people getting online, connecting, and collaborating with others both on and off the continent, learning and creating. What has happened is that as Internet penetration has increased, the playing field has been leveled and access to knowledge has increased. Africa has joined the knowledge economy and there are far less barriers to competing on this platform as opposed to other sectors of the economy.

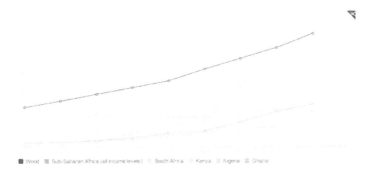

Figure 6: Internet users (per 100 people). Source: World Bank Open Data

Africa's youth are getting access to free and easily accessible sources of knowledge online. They are learning online what they sometimes cannot get in their classrooms, remixing that knowledge and producing new knowledge. The difference access to knowledge makes for a society or nation can be dramatic. For example, take the graph below which shows the difference in per capita incomes between Ghana and the Republic of Korea between 1960 and 2000 and the difference attributed to knowledge. While in 1960 the per capita incomes were more or less the same, in 40 years Korea increased its per capita income by a factor of 8.9 largely due to effective use of policy and technical knowledge while Ghana decreased by about 0.1.

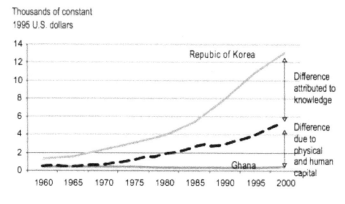

Source: World Bank, K4D program.

Figure 7: Difference between Ghana & Korean economies as a result of knowledge development

However, despite the great gains in recent years, Africa still has a long way to go. For example, out of the top 1 million websites globally, only 2,670 or 0.27% of those are hosted in Africa across only 34 out of 54 countries.

Social Africa

The growth of social networking in Africa has been unprecedented. In particular, Africa's youth have taken to Facebook rapidly and are engaging on social networks amongst themselves and their contemporaries across the globe. According to the latest statistics on socialbakers.com, Egypt leads the continent in terms of number of Facebook users with over 11 million users, a penetration rate of about 14% of the population. Nigeria comes in second with over 5 million Facebook users and a penetration rate of 3.3% of the total population and then South Africa which has close to 5 million Facebook users accounting for 10% of the population. In total there are currently just over 43 million Facebook users on the continent, a penetration rate of 4.63% of the population of the continent.

Mobile has played a significant role in the uptake of Facebook and other social networks such as Twitter on the continent and has also led to some innovative solutions. For example, ForgetMeNot Africa (FMNA) creates innovative solutions that bring the world of social networking to feature phones. With mobile being the device of choice on the continent but the majority of the devices being unconnected to the Internet, ForgetMeNot Africa's Optimiser Platform solves the problem of providing a wide range of internet services to these mobile phones, whether basic, feature or smart, using eTXTs.

Innovation Hubs

The numerous Innovation Hubs that have sprung up across the continent are the nerve centers of innovation. These spaces pioneered by Nairobi's Innovation Hub (iHub) are pooling together talented, innovative young people and creating a supportive environment for innovation. There are at least 35 tech hubs in 13 countries across Africa.

Innovation hubs have created amazing momentum in their areas of operation as far as creating centers that draw in talent, and nurture skills. Young people now have the opportunity to start and grow tech companies from the right environment. It is primarily in tech hubs that the startup culture is being 'incubated'.

These innovation hubs are especially instrumental at strengthening bottom of the pyramid innovations and startups - these are the scrappy startups which are at the pre-seed funding stage, where it's just a couple of people with an idea probably trying to come up with a prototype. The hub provides a place for these startups to work from without worrying about the basics such as office space or Internet connectivity and costs while at the same time being exposed to other like-minded individuals.

The hubs also create environments that support cross-pollination of ideas as developers meet and mix with designers and business people and eventually some amazing innovations can be born out of these environments.

In Silicon Valley, many great startups started in garages, the great startups of Africa will likely be born in these innovation hubs.

References:

The Next Big Thing: Africa, Dr. Dambisa Moyo, Foreign Policy, April 2009,
http://www.foreignpolicy.com/articles/2009/04/15/the_next_big_thing_africa

Sector Statistics Report Q2 2011-12, Communications Commission of Kenya,
http://www.cck.go.ke/resc/downloads/SECTOR_STATISTICS_REPORT_Q2_2011-12.pdf

Mobile Money Africa comes to Jo'burg,
http://www.southafrica.info/news/conferences/mobilemoneyafrica2012.htm

African Undersea Cables, Steve Song,
http://manypossibilities.net/african-undersea-cables/

Internet Usage Statistics for Africa, Internet World Stats,
http://www.internetworldstats.com/stats1.htm

Internet Users per 100 Inhabitants,
http://en.wikipedia.org/wiki/File:Internet_users_per_100_in
habitants_ITU.svg

The Google Global Cache Hits Kenya, Erik Hersman, April
2011, http://whiteafrican.com/2011/04/13/the-google-
global-cache-hits-kenya/

Local Web Cache Lessons: Uganda, Erik Hersman, January
2011, http://whiteafrican.com/2011/01/17/local-web-cache-
lessons-uganda/

Fostering Innovation, Productivity and Technological
Change: Tanzania in the Knowledge Economy, Anuj Utz,
http://info.worldbank.org/etools/docs/library/232302/Tanza
nia_in_the_Knowledge_Economy.pdf

Only 0.27% of the world's top 1 million sites are hosted in
Africa, Pingdom Blog, June 2012,
http://royal.pingdom.com/2012/06/27/tiny-percentage-of-
world-top-1-million-sites-hosted-africa/

Facebook Statistics, Social Bakers,
http://www.socialbakers.com/countries/continent-
detail/africa

Crowdsourcing Africa's tech hot-spots, 35 technology hubs mapped in 13 countries, Ben White, March 2012, http://vc4africa.biz/blog/2012/03/07/crowdsourcing-africas-tech-hot-spots-35-technology-hubs-mapped-in-13-countries/

Innovation Hubs and Small and Medium Enterprises in Africa: Setting the Policy Agenda, Dorothy McCormick and Jackson Maalu, http://www.aibuma.org/proceedings2011/aibuma2011-submission233.pdf

Afropolitans: The face of a modernizing Africa, Euromonitor International, July 2010, http://blog.euromonitor.com/2010/07/afropolitans-the-face-of-a-modernising-africa.html

Insights Africa: Explore the media habits of consumers in Sub-Saharan Africa,

http://www.insightsafrica.com/

The Next Frontier in Innovation in Africa
By Mbwana Alliy

The African technology scene has never been more exciting. As the continent's approximately 1 billion strong population gets comes online primarily through mobile, Africa offers a truly "mobile first" opportunity. While the "mobile first" meme is common in places such as Silicon Valley as a specific strategy to address the transition into a mobile-centric computing world, Africa is leading the way as far as the radical transformation of societies through mobile technology. For example, despite the fact that the mobile money in Africa story has been cited over and over again by press and analysts, its effect on reshaping African economies and showing the world what a truly mobile first continent can unleash in terms of innovation is just beginning.

Innovation may come from almost any sector or discipline. Take Leila Janah who organized the first Facebook Developer Garage in East Africa in 2008 (way before the wave of interest in Africa as a place where technology innovation and entrepreneurship could thrive really took root). Her colleagues and friends back at Silicon Valley must have thought she was mad! Now, she is leading the revolution in microwork (getting small tasks such as tagging images done over the Internet) through her organization Samasource, proving that there are opportunities in technology even for the bottom of the pyramid.

Fast-forward to today and many social venture funds and budding social enterprises recognize the power of technology, and specifically the web and mobile, as powerful catalysts for change. The most powerful thing about these social entrepreneurs is that they bring top global talent into a much needed sector and often hold up a mirror to both diaspora Africans and resident Africans alike, showing that there are opportunities for real lasting change that can be brought about by leveraging technology and innovation. The question now is more who will shape it and who will be part of this new reality for Africa.

Where will the next innovation to benefit Africa originate?

There are two main schools of thoughts here:

1. Technology Transfer: Africa Consumes what the Rest of the World Produces

This postulates that Africans are primarily consumers of technology. Dominant technologies spread from the west (Silicon Valley and other places) outwards with Africans primarily consuming the benefits while perhaps doing minor modifications to adapt the technology to the context.

African's are however proving more and more that they are not just passive consumers of foreign technology. They can contribute something and even export homegrown technology to the rest of the world. Here are just three examples of this:

i. Ushahidi: is a non-profit software company that develops free and open source software for information collection, visualization and interactive mapping. The organization originated with the development of their primary product 'Ushahidi', a web-based tool for crowdsourcing and mapping critical information in crisis situations for the purpose of aiding rescue operations, for example. Originally developed by a primarily Kenyan community of developers, the founders went on to create the company, which now produces other products. Ushahidi has been used all over the world, from Haiti during the fatal January 2010 earthquake, to the catastrophic 2011 Japan earthquake and has been used by media agencies such as the Washington Post and Al Jazeera.

ii. Ubuntu Linux: Probably the most popular distribution of the Linux operating system, Ubuntu was started by Mark Shuttleworth a South African entrepreneur.

iii. MPESA: MPESA is the premier and most successful mobile money service that hailed out of Kenya and was deployed by Safaricom, Kenya's biggest Mobile Network Operator. The mobile money industry has grown significantly since the introduction and success of MPESA in Kenya; mobile money has been introduced to many other countries.

2. Innovation loves constraints: Africa is well suited for innovation in technology

The other school of thought is that innovation can come from anywhere really; that in fact "innovation loves constraints" and "frugal innovation" – achieving more with less resources - can lead to the next breakthrough to help the next billion people and emerging middle class participate in the technology revolution. As Erik Hersman, co-founder of the afore-mentioned Ushahidi, once noted "*If it works in Africa, it will work anywhere*" – the point he was trying to make really is that innovating in Africa places so many constraints on the innovator and the innovation process is very likely to produce a "battle-hardened" product, so to speak.

Most are increasingly supporting the latter view that Africa and Africans can and should be active players in innovating technologies.

With the falling cost of launching internet scale applications thanks to cloud computing and open source software, gone are the days when big budgets and big R&D centers were required to do research. Everything from commerce to health and bioinformatics can increasingly be done in a distributed manner. With undersea cables bringing connectivity, fast 3G and LTE/4G networks expanding into Africa and even investments in Supercomputing clusters such as that led by the Nairobi Innovation Hub (iHub), the necessary infrastructure is in place setting the stage for Africa-centric, "leap frogging", innovation.

Africans who have never left the continent tend to have a mindset challenge as a result of outdated tertiary and even secondary education systems. Organizations such as the Africa Leadership Academy (ALA) in South Africa and Ghana's Ashesi University that are taking innovative approaches to educating the next generation of African leaders in many disciplines including technology, as well as the many technology and innovation hubs that have sprung up across the continent in recent times are filling that critical gap in reshaping the mindsets of young Africans. Role models are finally emerging with a distinct and unique message. Take Tony Elumelu, for example, an inspiring Nigerian who has built a banking empire and is also a philanthropist. He coined the term *Africapitalism,* referring to an economic philosophy that embodies the private sector's commitment to the economic transformation of Africa through investments that create both economic prosperity and social wealth.

The Silicon Valley elite, with their massive wealth resources have been a huge force behind the idea of social or philanthro-venture capital. Their goals are primarily the creation of social change but using the business techniques they've honed in Silicon Valley. Take for instance Omidyar Network, the investment firm set up by eBay founder Pierre

Omidyar that supported Ushahidi and kick-started the innovation hub revolution across the continent that started with the iHub in Kenya.

What is the best way to fund, nurture and support innovators?

There are three distinct approaches that are currently being undertaken to searching, funding and scaling the next innovation.

1. AID: Africa has had a long history of mostly failed AID policies. Many foreign aid organizations are now retooling themselves to run innovation prizes or creating innovation funds.

2. The Social Venture/Social Entrepreneurship model

3. Private-sector backed initiatives

Each of these models has their merits and downfalls. For instance, it is not clear whether the Social Venture model is taking enough risk to seed early stage innovations and it's also not clear whether grant financing comes with the right technical and managerial support in addition to the money. It's very easy to muddle and confuse early stage risk capital with "free but dumb" money from grants i.e. funding that doesn't help educate, connect and build up the entrepreneur, or worse still comes with strings attached. On the other hand, if a social innovation is proven to work, Social Venture funds have the resources to help fund and sustain it.

The private sector that was largely absent in funding innovation (in Africa) in a traditional venture capital model is increasingly present at all levels including the seed stage. However it's not clear whether the total funding ecosystem may ever get to be as good as it is in Silicon Valley, for instance. There are other alternatives though; crowd funding, for instance, could be one of the ways to bridge the funding gap for innovators and entrepreneurs in Africa.

The often not talked about missing piece is the hands-on technical expertise in the form of accomplished tech entrepreneurs turned angel investors. In Africa, they tend to be very few, isolated, and alone or fragmented, as opposed to more mature networks such as those within Silicon Valley. But can there be a direct bridge from the mature ecosystem to developing ones in Africa without tying into outdated funding models? For example, I/O Ventures is an early stage startup accelerator founded by Paul Bragiel, a serial entrepreneur from Silicon Valley; in 2010, I/O

Ventures led a trip to East Africa that led to connections being made with the Tanzanian Government at the presidential level as well as with the Kenya ICT Board. The trip created the opportunity through which the needs of these governments and nations (as far as creating startup and innovation ecosystems) could be brought up and opened avenues for providing mentoring and policy assistance based on direct experience.

In reality, it might actually be a mix or hybrid of models that actually helps African innovation take off. For instance, M-PESA, the pioneering mobile money solution, got started as a result of a Department for International Development (DFID – the UK development organization) grant for a pilot to Vodafone. Ultimately it was Safaricom, the Kenyan telecom giant, through its agent model that helped scale the service to millions of Kenyans. This scaling would have been hampered had the Kenyan Government decided to step in very early on and aggressively regulate mobile money (a strategy undertaken by Nigeria). These intricacies can have a real effect on the spread of the benefits of innovation. Attempts to replicate M-PESA have had mixed success rates - in Tanzania, for example, it was only after a $5M Gates Foundation grant to Vodacom, for marketing technical assistance, that M-PESA finally not only took off, but also fueled a very competitive mobile money industry - even more competitive than in Kenya where Safaricom is a dominant monopoly with less incentive for innovation around the model they scaled.

Social Enterprise and Funding

The question has been raised often: *What exactly qualifies as "social innovation" and how do you tell it apart from a for profit innovation?*

Take the case of M-PESA as an example once more: the service is operated as a commercial endeavor now, but got its start through a grant. Furthermore, despite being a for-profit undertaking, it is hard to decouple M-PESA from the real social benefits that have been accrued as a result – call it "banking the unbanked" or "financial inclusion".

Making the distinction can make a real difference to the entrepreneur: Where should the entrepreneur start looking for funding and support for their idea? Should they label themselves as social entrepreneurs because there is the perception that there is a lot of capital in this sector and hence can maximize chances of funding outcome?

Looking at the for profit side, in Africa, we have seen a low success rate so far, in terms of technology startups that have gone on to become large commercial enterprises that have reached what the west might deem "success", via a windfall liquidity; events such as an Initial Public Offer (IPO) or mergers & acquisitions (M&A) - Of course, The situation is bound to change in time as more players come in and the ecosystem matures – more startups, more funding sources, more successes etc.

The level of private equity funding directed at growth and expansion stage for companies continues to increase even though, at least in tech, the seed financing side of the equation is yet to be adequately addressed. This, in part, has prompted the donor community to enter the early stage tech market in an attempt to fill the void. Such actions by the donor community have the potential risk of crowding out private investors who do exist but are not yet visible. Worse yet, donors tend to focus on prize money and competitions where 'cool' apps are more likely to take home the prize as opposed to a wholistic view that takes into account product viability, the existence of an addressable market and the ease with which that market can be accessed, sound financials and overall business model. This can result in a lot of hype generation whereas upon review by real market investors the product or service may not meet the standard. Winning awards or competitions in tech in Africa may actually damage the innovation funding ecosystem because many of these competitions don't do the job of actually supporting, mentoring and filtering out poor products or services while picking out those with real market potential and helping them get to the next level - an idea is not the same as working and sustainable service. Similarly with the boom in workspaces, incubators and accelerators, how many of them have really built a tech community of investors, mentors and corporations who care about the ecosystem versus only achieving short term goals?

There is a perception in the west that the venture capital model is broken as it hasn't lived up to expectations in the face of less successful IPOs. So why would a broken venture capital model in the west work in Africa? There are alternatives to the standard models - take a look at Kenya, for example, and you will find an undercurrent of homegrown private equity via so-called "*Chamas*" (savings and investment groups) that has built out success stories such as Equity Bank and been quite active in real estate. Are we at a point where these homegrown groups might participate in helping fund homegrown tech innovations in the spirit that only Africans can build Africa?

References:

So you want to be the Silicon Valley of Africa?, Mbwana Alliy, Afrinnovator, November 2010, http://afrinnovator.com/blog/2010/11/01/so-you-want-to-be-the-silicon-valley-of-africa/

Silicon Valley to mentor Dar es Salaam's ICT sector, IPP Media, http://www.ippmedia.com/frontend/index.php?l=20383

Connecting Tanzania to Silicon Valley, Mbwana Alliy, http://www.mbwana.com/uploads/8/0/4/8/8048875/io_f-study.pdf

Africapitalism, http://heirsholdings.com/africapitalism

How Tony Elumelu's 'Africapitalism' Aims to Redefine African Economic Development, Tracy Elsen, http://www.nextbillion.net/blogpost.aspx?blogid=2780

Vodacom gets US $4.8 million to expand M-Pesa services, http://www.vodacom.co.tz/about-us/news/2010/11/vodacom-gets-us-$48-million-to-expand-m-pesa-services-

African Leadership University, http://www.africanleadershipacademy.org/

Ashesi University, http://www.ashesi.edu.gh/

A Brief History of Ubuntu,
http://www.informit.com/articles/article.aspx?p=1186095&
seqNum=3

Ushahidi, http://ushahidi.com

Doing Tech Business in Africa: A Few Lessons from Twitter's Rise in Africa

By Will Mutua

Earlier this year, Portland Communications, a communications consultancy company, released their research findings on the usage of Twitter in Africa. The report was received quite well and received some notable attention across the web. What insights about doing tech business/startups in Africa can we glean from this research?

Qualitative vs. Quantitative Factors

According to the report, South Africa is the continent's most active country by volume of geo-located Tweets, with over twice as many Tweets (5,030,226 during Q4 2011) as the next most active Kenya (2,476,800) and third comes Nigeria at 1,646,212 tweets. This continues to give credence to the idea that these three are the countries to watch as far as technology and innovation in Africa go. Looking at rankings based on World Bank and International Finance Corporation (IFC) data, these three countries feature prominently among the top 15 countries in Sub-Saharan Africa that are easiest to do business in –

South Africa ranks 2nd, Kenya 9th and Nigeria 15th. This shows that there's a correlation between which countries tech startups are likely to succeed and their macro-economic situation.

Rank	Country
1	Mauritius
2	South Africa
3	Rwanda
4	Botswana
5	Ghana
6	Namibia
7	Zambia
8	Seychelles
9	Kenya
10	Ethiopia

Table 1: Top 10 countries in Africa by ease of doing business, Data Source: World Bank,
http://doingbusiness.org

It is interesting, however, that based largely on more quantifiable terms such as taxation and credit rankings, the latter two of these three countries do not appear to be the most promising to invest in a tech startup relative to others on the list. There appears to be other factors that make these countries rise above other states that would seem obviously better candidates when considering where to establish a tech startup than these, at least by looking at the economic indicators.

It seems more qualitative aspects have a strong bearing on where to conduct tech business in Africa. Two key qualitative considerations are:

An entrepreneurial support network – Startup Culture:

Basically is there a critical mass of other like-minded people in the country? People you can learn from, people who've already interacted with the system and have learnt how to go about things in that country when doing tech business? In any case, having more people trying to achieve in the same area as you are also makes it exciting to do business and creates a great ecosystem to operate in.

Perhaps that's why so many tech startups move to Silicon Valley, there's something about being in a place where there are many people competing and cooperating. Such clusters also create great feeding grounds for investors. Vibrant innovation hubs such as Nairobi's Innovation Hub and Nigeria's Co-Creation Hub are indicative of the presence of a strong entrepreneurial support network.

Lesson: Don't forget the qualitative aspects. Balance out the quantitative aspects verses the more qualitative ones.

Culture

It can be devastating for foreign investors to fall into the misunderstanding that Africa is one country, with one culture. The fact of the matter is that the African continent is diverse and this diversity has far-reaching implications not only on how to relate to people but also how people prefer to do business in different parts of Africa.

The business culture in some countries is really fast-paced and aggressive whilst in other areas there's a kind of laid-back, easy-going culture (which does not necessarily indicate that there are less opportunities in such a culture, or that the people there are not as entrepreneurial). Investors need to take time to study their chosen country for investment and understand what the people are like, what their culture is like, then adapt, and approach investments with that understanding.

Local culture also has an impact on how consumers respond to products – not just the product itself but how it is presented and the messaging around it. You can have a great product and kill it with your advertising messaging.

A great example of how understanding the culture can make a great difference in how well the target market take up a product in Kenya is Safaricom's advertising. Many of Safaricom's products have been more widely received than competing offerings simply because they have understood local Kenyan lingo and incorporated it in product names and advertising messaging.

For example, transferring airtime credit from one's Safaricom line to another is dubbed "*Sambaza*"; the competing Airtel service called their own similar offering "ME2U" (a mistake of Airtel's predecessors, Airtel seems to be doing much better at their messaging) People took to *Sambaza* versus *ME2U* and nowadays you'll hear a Kenyan with an Airtel line saying they want to "Sambaza" credit to another Airtel line… this is exactly the same thing as saying you are going to "'*Google something on Yahoo*"

Still on the issue of culture, foreign investors also need to understand that Africa is a unique playing ground. Do not approach Africa with the idea that things will work here the same way they work elsewhere in the world just because they work in those other places. In fact, going back to the issue of the rich diversity of the continent, one strategy may not even work for two different countries *within* Africa, *even in the same region*!

With the diversity of the continent comes the uniqueness of states and regions within the continent.

These two amazing qualities of the African continent are in part contributed to by the histories of the different states, whilst many African states got their independence from colonial masters around the same period in history, their experience of colonialism, and other factors including their pre-colonial history, set them on vastly different tracks in some cases.

Lesson: Keep in mind the context of your operation

The Youth of Africa are where it's at!

The Twitter report indicates that 60% of Africa's tweeters are between the ages of 20 and 29.

According to the 2011 Africa Youth Report compiled by the Economic Commission for Africa:

"The majority of Africa's population is below the age of 30... Young Africans are the key to an African renaissance and will remain players in and advocates of social transformation and development in many spheres. The

enormous benefits young people can contribute are realized when investment is made in young people's education, employment, health care, empowerment and effective civil participation."

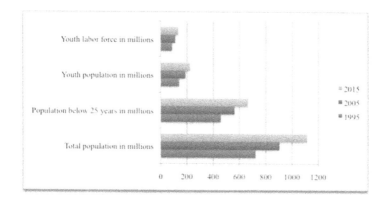

Figure 8: African population, youth population and labor force. Source International Labor Organization (ILO) Economically Active Population and Projections (EAPAP) database

Almost two-thirds of the population in Africa is below 25 years of age. More than 20 per cent, or almost 189 million, are youth between 15 and 24 years of age. This share will remain more or less constant for the next 10 years.

This presents an unprecedented market and labor pool if tapped. Many are tech savvy and connected unlike ever before on the African continent and are willing to learn and to try new things. They do not have immediate memory of colonial times, and so are not living with that burden on their minds; they see a world open to them to explore, where they can compete, share with and learn from their contemporaries across the globe. Thanks to the Internet and World Wide Web, (particularly delivered via mobile) they have ready access to information and this has empowered them.

Lesson: Tap into the youthful African population

Reflecting again on the Twitter report, it is interesting that majority of Twitter users in Africa are using it to stay connected with friends – 81% of those polled saying that they mainly used Twitter for communication with friends. One could easily draw a parallel between Twitter and SMS messaging (only that Tweeting is cheaper). Perhaps one reason why Twitter is picking up is that Africans can already relate to sending short messages via mobile and so it is really easy to turn to the Internet for communication with friends – the principle is the same.

Lesson: If you're introducing something new, it could be helpful if you can mimic something that's already common to increase adoption rate

The Power of Mobile

The Portland Communications research indicates that close to 60% of tweets from Africa are sent via mobile phone. Now, the amazing link between Africa and the mobile platform is not a new subject, but one that deserves mention over and over again. The simple fact is that the mobile device will remain the most powerful platform to reach the mass market in Africa for some time to come.

There are companies that are doing pretty well by tapping into this. For example, ForgetMeNot Africa brings Internet messaging and social networking to every mobile phone including the most basic 'feature' phones without WAP.

References:

How Africa Tweets, Portland Communications, http://www.portland-communications.com/Twitter_in_Africa_PPT.pdf

Ranking of economies based on ease of doing business, IFC & World Bank, http://www.doingbusiness.org/rankings

Pondering Africa's Tech Investment Potential in 2012 and Beyond, Will Mutua, http://afrinnovator.com/blog/2012/01/15/pondering-africas-tech-investment-potential-in-2012-and-beyond/

African Youth Report 2011, UNECA,
http://www.uneca.org/ayr2011/African%20Youth%20Report_2011_Final.pdf

Kenya Julisha ICT Report: Invest in New Skills, Mbwana Alliy, http://afrinnovator.com/blog/2011/11/24/kenya-julisha-ict-report-invest-in-new-skills-its-called-human-capital/

Let's Unleash SMS: Africa's best distribution platform, Mbwana Alliy,
http://afrinnovator.com/blog/2011/11/13/insights-sms-is-africas-best-distribution/

Forecasting Africa's Mobile Future, Will Mutua,
http://afrinnovator.com/blog/2011/11/09/forecasting-africas-mobile-future/

http://forgetmenotafrica.com/

Which African country is best to do a tech startup? A Decision Framework

By Mbwana Alliy

Africa is a diverse continent, 54 countries and a wide array of cultures. A few countries, namely Nigeria, Kenya and South Africa have been touted as the technology hubs of Africa. But are they really the *only* ones where one can succeed at doing a tech startup in Africa? Certainly not. So how do you determine the best places on the continent to do a tech startup?

There is no one right answer – the following is a decision framework based on real data and trends - this should help people assess their situation and move forward and get on with their startup. However picking a country to launch should not be taken lightly. This framework (more questions to ask yourself) can act as a guide to assess at each stage what is practical - for instance you may grow up in one country, but your needs mean you have to move to another country to take advantage of further opportunities.

What kind of startup organization are you trying to build?

Answering this question should get most people halfway to deciding where to do any startup and that includes tech. Each country in Africa has a unique offering for the kind of company you are trying to build. If you are importing materials or products you may want to be near a port such as Dar es Salaam or Mombasa. Which one is easiest to deal with? Which one offers the best road network to move your products? If you intend to build a tourism-related company you may want to be in an area with all the safari tour operators and major attractions; it's also easier to hire talent that understand the tourism industry.

Look for strong macro-economic factors - *but the right ones.*

On the surface, the best countries in Africa for a tech startup are simply the ones with the best internet and mobile penetration figures, large middle class populations and fastest growing economies (GDP-wise), these include South Africa, Nigeria, Ghana, Egypt. But this is sometimes limiting.

The 2010 McKinsey Global Institute report on Africa's economies, *"Lions on the move: The progress and potential of African economies"*, provides a great framework for analyzing and classifying Africa's economies at a broad level. The four general classifications are:

- **Diverse Economies**: Africa's growth engines and her most advanced economies – Egypt, Tunisia, Morocco, South Africa.

- **Oil Exporters**: Economies that are overly dependent on oil export. They have the highest GDPs but the least diversification. Algeria, Angola and Nigeria being the largest of these.

- **Transition Economies**: Lower GDP than the previous two, but growing rapidly with agriculture and resources accounting for up to 35% of GDP, they're also exporting more manufactured goods particularly to other African countries.

- **Pre-transition Economies**: Very poor; generally lack strong, stable governments and macroeconomic conditions.

Exports per capita show the raw output and productivity of a country; the diversity of the economy essentially shows how much a country depends on mineral resources. Both taken together are extremely important and can help drive decisions. An economy that is overly dependent on oil exports, for example, can be a problem. How? Well, it drives the expectations of that country and internal economy dynamics. A lot of talent is in the petroleum economy, why should talented folks leave and join your startup with no revenues when they can make more working in the established industry? Money aside, maybe that programmer you are trying to hire in Nigeria would never leave that oil company because their parents expect him to get a steady job (in Oil), find a nice wife and settle down.

This also applies to a country's dependence on AID. Some countries are so dependent on AID, which makes up as much as half the economy, which can have far-reaching economic implications.

An African country historically concentrated too much on one industry (especially natural resources such as oil- look up resource curse) can be very negative on their economy for trying new things and tech is all about new ways of doing business and efficiency.

Consider South Africa - no wonders over half of African investment in private equity ends up there; it's a big country, well diversified with high export earnings. It's hard not to consider South Africa for a tech startup on the continent. But even this masks other considerations before one jumps into a country.

If you are building a social enterprise and raising impact-investing capital, you may actually benefit from looking at other metrics beyond which countries are best performing economically. For example, which countries have the most NEED and hence your possible impact? For instance, where are the highest Malaria infection rates if you are doing an mHealth app around this problem? The countries that have the most need tend to be the ones that have the worst macro-economic conditions. For example, Malaria has been said to be responsible for 1% negative GDP growth that African countries have experienced in the last 50 years - no wonder Bill Gates is investing his money to make an impact in this area.

Watch for barriers, regulatory environment that might open or block market access to a country that might otherwise look lucrative

Despite the concerns about economic diversification, when looking at raw market size, numbers can also be deceiving. Nigeria is absolutely the single biggest African market right now with a population of 160M and with over half that with mobile phones, it's indeed lucrative. But down the line, the East African Community (EAC) presents a potential 120M people between the member countries Tanzania, Kenya, Uganda, Burundi and Rwanda - and a possible single currency soon.

Size of a single country is not the only thing that matters, market access does. Take mobile banking as an example: in Kenya you have 15M people mobile users with M-PESA and 7 transactions a second. Whilst in Nigeria, there are supposedly 11 mobile banking companies that are operating and the regulatory environment meant that they had to apply for those licenses. The potential for mobile money in Nigeria is certainly huge, but it's still very early. Without a strong agent network and being so fragmented, it's hard for mobile money to see the growth and success that Kenya does right now. Regulation has hindered the growth of mobile banking thus far, and once licenses were released, 11 services jumped into the market. That being said, Nigeria is forecasted to hit 20M mobile banking users by 2015.

Another example on regulation is Tanzania's very odd 18% VAT phone tax which has been abandoned by neighboring countries. What is strange is that there are no such taxes on traditional PCs! Phone manufacturers like Nokia and Samsung absolutely hate this since it denies them a chance to sell higher profit margin phones where they will make their money in the future. The point is that Tanzania smartphone penetration, which is strongly correlated to mobile web access, may remain stubbornly low compared to its neighbors. And the data, when digging deeper shows this (but of course, other factors are in play, like the higher GDP per capita). New Government stats show that whilst Kenya only just edges Tanzania in mobile penetration (68% vs. 45%), the web penetration gap is much wider by 3 times (36% vs. 11%).

Support network, doing business & entrepreneurial ecosystem

Simple things such as finding a qualified and fairly priced lawyer can present significant challenge in some countries, or how easy it is to register your business (especially as a foreigner), get a bank account and other such things.

Similarly, closer to tech, hubs are now popping up all over the continent; it is now getting "cooler" to hang out at these spaces and bump into like-minded people in a community setting, peer-to-peer networking as well as regular visits from investors and tech industry, mentors and officials. In short, tech workspaces such as the iHub in Nairobi or the Co-Creation Hub in Nigeria backed by the industry make doing business in technology much easier, not to mention bringing legitimacy to the tech scene in the country. A fragmented tech scene does not help investors and like-minded people trying to connect with each other. South Africa, for example, has a number of spaces and initiatives around the 'Silicon Cape' that coupled with appropriate talent foster faster launching of startups.

Another factor of the ecosystem relates to expectations of investors and valuation of technology and startups. Because of the understanding of technology's impact in the economy, some investors make unreasonable demands on startups such as asking for 50% equity stake of a business for a very small valuation. Closely related is the willingness and comfort of big companies to buy startups at decent valuations to provide a return to investors and especially the entrepreneur for taking the risk in doing a startup. We have seen little to almost none of this appreciation in Africa to date, but global companies like Visa with the recent acquisition of Fundamo, one of the biggest vendors of mobile financial services technology, may begin to pave the way. You can bet that technology startups will disrupt banking, media and other industries in Africa as the Internet has in the rest of world. The question is, how quickly do the incumbent companies recognize this and pay for innovation or suffer a death from the disruption? Countries that encourage this and hence coordinate the entire ecosystem end to end will have a more dynamic IT industry.

Competitive Dynamics

Whilst, say, Tanzania may not be as business friendly as neighboring Kenya, there are generally less competitors in that market for any given sector. This can be a significant advantage. (Note that in the EAC case such advantages may eventually erode away just as it happened in the Euro as free movement of labor, capital and goods makes it easier to transact across the region.)

At the same time lack of competition is also a bad thing, especially where there is scarcity of support services such as qualified lawyers or relevantly skilled engineering talent. You might find the few qualified and skilled individuals might demand a premium for their services.

Unique industry advantages & Startup Lifestyle

Take Tanzania as an example again: if working in Dar es Salaam, one can easily take a $10 2-hour ferry ride or $70 flight in 20 minutes and be in total paradise, away from work, in Zanzibar. "Getting away from it all" can be crucial to maintaining a good work-life balance. This is one of the reasons why the Silicon Valley is so great. It has amazing weather and offers access to a variety of outdoor activities; you can go snowboarding one day and surf the next.

Another factor related to lifestyle is the expectations of the startup and founders' ambitions. Some investors claim that in many parts of the emerging market too many entrepreneurs have aspirations to build a family business and have no expectations that their investors from whom they raised money may want to exit at some point. VCs don't fund family businesses; they are looking for big regional, if not global businesses. The sort of startup life you want and whom you want to draw investments from can impact where you need to be. This point is closely related to *"the kind of organization you want to build"*, which in turn informs the sort of investor you want to attract and ultimately where you are likely to find this.

Be Global: Take advantage of all the countries and their diversities.

The best startups treat the world as flat, and from day one are opportunistic about where they source customers, talent and investors. The most diverse, networked entrepreneurs will do best. Apple designs and markets in California and manufactures in China; tablets can be designed in Nigeria and manufactured in China too. Let's promote more regional trade within Africa to help each other out. It is exciting that Kenya's M-PESA has inspired other startups and even big companies to try replicate their success around the continent.

One country that stands out a lot for financial access, doing business and transacting across the continent and Indian subcontinent is Mauritius. It offers some of the best tax advantages thanks to its treaties with numerous African countries and has transformed itself as a financial hub; a lot of it has to do with its political stability over the years, as well as a government push to be able to do this (note: it's a very diversified economy based on the chart above). Botswana, with its International Financial Services Centre is trying to be a financial hub too, given similar advantages and ambitions. Perhaps startups that grow to substantial size and start expanding across the region might think about reincorporating their startups in hubs such as Mauritius, Botswana or South Africa, especially if there is a remote chance of getting acquired by a multinational company or they want to float on a public exchange via an IPO.

Conclusion

Given what we've seen so far, it is evident that there is a lot of diversity and no one country is the only place to launch a startup.

As a final note: almost always, entrepreneurs need to intimately understand all these factors in any chosen country and, in particular, people who can guide them through the unique environment. Many emerging market countries, including those in Africa, have unique cultural and business practices that are best understood by working closely with trusted people.

References:

Lions on the move: The progress and potential of African economies, McKinsey Global Institute, http://www.mckinsey.com/insights/mgi/research/productivi ty_competitiveness_and_growth/lions_on_the_move

East Africa may adopt single currency this year, Daily Nation online, http://www.nation.co.ke/business/news/East+Africa+may+ adopt+single+currency+this+year/-/1006/1305588/- /yr8kex/-/index.html

Nigeria to become dominant in Africa's mobile payment market, Business Day Online, http://www.businessdayonline.com/NG/index.php/news/76 -hot-topic/31507--nigeria-to-become-dominant-in-africas- mobile-payment-market

Tanzania: Tax Rises Will Impede Growth of Telecom Industry, Govt Told, Al-Amani Mutarubukwa, http://allafrica.com/stories/201106090501.html

Mobile Technology in Tanzania, Leo Mutuku,
http://www.ihub.co.ke/blog/2012/01/mobile-technology-in-tanzania/

Co-Creation Hub Nigeria, http://www.cchubnigeria.com/

Innovation House Opened in Silicon Valley,
http://www.norway.org/News_and_events/Research--Technology/Innovation-House-Opened-in-Silicon-Valley/

The Road Ahead: Blueprint for Building Africa's Tech Ecosystem

By Mbwana Alliy

The modern technology Ecosystem of Silicon Valley is a well-oiled machine that keeps on producing innovations that impact the world. In the last few years, the Valley culture has been slowly spreading across the world. Call it the globalization of Silicon Valley. More and more people are recognizing tech opportunities around the world.

Now, it's Africa's turn! It is now impossible to ignore the strong economic growth and other indicators that point to not only a larger African consumer market and middle class, but also a more connected continent that makes it easier to reach and serve Africans even if many are still classed as "bottom of the pyramid". Thanks to undersea cables that have brought down the cost of communications and internet starting from mid last decade, and now conferences and pitch contests following on the heels of the establishment of numerous workspaces and hubs on the continent, Africa is facing a new era that is arguably only limited by 3 challenges:

1. *Africa's perception and legacy:* Despite the progress we are seeing in Africa, legacy and perception issues hold back investment and awareness in the tech sector. Governments overly focus on real estate and infrastructure vs. talent development and policies to encourage foreign investors and business friendly environments to allow tech startups to thrive.

2. ***Ability to develop homegrown talent through the right technical, managerial and entrepreneurial education***: The explosion of workspaces in Africa is actually quite easy to explain: Africa once felt like a very fragmented tech ecosystem. You might be the only person in Zambia who codes in python and you feel isolated, you will get nowhere unless you try find like-minded people and the network of investors and mentors to realize your potential. Furthermore, your tech skills are not well appreciated. Career distractions and traditional paths in a non-tech region make it harder for someone to benefit from their intrinsic interest in technology. The hubs are filling in the gap by aggregating talent, and creating opportunities for learning and sharing skills, as well as

entrepreneurial thinking. Borrowing from the popular song, "Young Man, Go to the YMCA!" for the Nairobi techie it increasingly sounds like *"Young Man, Go to the iHub!"*.

3. *Opportunity cost of investing in other sectors vs. Tech*: Similar to talent in tech, many investors in Africa can and continue to enjoy great returns in areas such as commodities and real estate, where growth can be as much as 30% a year, making return on investment and payback periods very attractive as compared to tech. Tech requires patience and the risk-return profile is very different from other businesses, especially when you couple that with the fact that many investors are neither patient nor tech savvy. This, however, will change as investors realize the market opportunity and instant distribution to consumers that technology enables, but many will remain late-stage investors due to the current structure of their funds. The early stage funding problem will remain a problem as long as there isn't any tech savvy angel network that is willing to take risks and roll up their sleeves to get their hands dirty. What about exits you say? It's not like Silicon Valley where "acqhires" offer

investors downside protection by tapping next-door cash-rich tech companies looking for talent to allow them to continue to innovate. The challenge in Africa remains finding entrepreneurs who bet big to build solid, scalable businesses or innovations across the region to generate exit potential as well as educating regional corporations and investors on the importance of tech in their business if they are not to be left behind.

Despite these challenges, a few observations offer great hope as to why we are only beginning and will see a continued acceleration of Africa's tech ecosystem as these barriers come down and challenges get solved.

Reconfiguring of AID systems to Philanthro-capitalism

AID has the fuel that propped up governments and NGOs historically without contributing to economic growth. Dr. Dambisa Moyo in her book, 'Dead Aid', does a great job of enumerating the demerits of the AID system. Did the BRIC countries lift themselves out of poverty thanks to the World Bank or was it their own style of capitalism and development? Organizations such as the Tony Elumelu

Foundation with its "Africapitalism" campaign are the trailblazers, showing how to build economies in Africa.

Aid often crowds out private investment as well. So with less money going into these aid channels, legacy institution's influence is now waning. Technology is becoming a key ingredient in social innovations and many governments in Africa are starting to recognize their importance and increasingly building tech capacity.

It used to be that a retired tech executive or newly minted rich entrepreneur in the western world with a curiosity about Africa would start a non-profit or donate to one. They still can, but there are new avenues and tools to find and achieve a wider choice of impact. Now they can put the same money into angel investing (with increasingly less capital needed for tech startups) or contribute to an impact fund. For example, Salesforce, a global enterprise software company, has pioneered an interesting CSR model and is actively engaged in social ventures. With the rise of clicktivism, (take the Kony 2012 campaign as an example, though not the best), we will begin to see more technology-based efforts put into solving Africa's social problems.

The role of Diaspora and expats in bringing the skills and talents to Africa

Many economies in the West are experiencing a period of economic uncertainty. This provides ample opportunity for talent to address a new spectrum of tech problems in other geographies.

Them that understand how things work in Africa can start addressing opportunities that no one else is, impacting millions of people in the process and make money doing it. The African diaspora has a critical role to play here; they have the exposure and experience of studying and working off the continent, yet they are well placed to understand the nuances of the continent.

New models of education and mentoring paired with risk capital

Accelerator models with technical and managerial networks help prepare first-time entrepreneurs at much lower risk with low amounts of capital, even if more than half of the companies fail (a lesson in failure is a powerful thing, plus, the alumni they create provide a valuable talent pool in subsequent years for the successful startups to draw upon). Silicon Valley's no exception; you will find folks who tried a startup for a year that failed, yet the next year they are directly managing a $1M a year businesses upon joining a successful startup that has achieved escape velocity. A culture that accepts failure is critical to innovation and Silicon Valley thrives in it every day. There's even a conference called 'FailCon' in the Valley for technology entrepreneurs, investors, developers and designers to study their own and others' failures and hence prepare for success!

New financing models such as crowdfunding are only made possible thanks to online distribution and global participation platforms enabled by tech. This means that ideas can be turned into prototypes and subsequently floated for funding on such platforms faster than ever before. It, however, takes investors who are willing to come in early, be patient, and are not put off by failure. Lessons from failure can help seed a wealth of experience from which future entrepreneurs can draw lessons, thereby avoiding common pitfalls and hence increasing the chances for success. Hands-on investing in Africa is becoming a reality as the talent and markets around technology continue to develop. Well-run incubators challenge the very notion of educational systems to prepare future entrepreneurs. Take, as an example, the cases of the so-called 'Paypal Mafia' or the Y-Combinator Alumni who are already forming a formidable network in the Valley.

It seems every day we are hearing more positive news on Africa's tech scene, we now need more success stories of breakthrough companies and products beyond Ushahidi and M-PESA. We are right at the cusp of that breakthrough; the blueprint has been laid - we must keep building, and remember, it's ok to fail if you learn and move forward.

	PERCEPTION & LEGACY	DEVELOPING TALENT	INVESTMENT
THE PAST	Aid Systems crowd out private investors. Political instability and high-perceived investment risk.	Weak tertiary education and training systems = lack of talent to support a thriving homegrown tech ecosystem.	Return on Investment and Payback period attractive in other sector e.g. commodities Boom, Real Estate etc...
	Can't serve the "poor" in Africa except through charity.		Traditional Private Equity/VC structures favor high minimum investment in business with proven business models
THE FUTURE	Africa is the last big consumer and has the fastest-growing middle class.	Incubators, Accelerators and Hubs/Workspaces + Tech events/pitch contests act as finishing schools and readiness for Entrepreneurs. These are the new Universities that facilitate peer learning, learning from failure.	Tech recognized as key drivers to economy thanks to investment in infrastructure and rise of connected African consumer. Instant Distribution and payment systems develop at scale.
	"Arab Spring Moment" acts as a reset. Entrepreneurship recognized as key to stability and prosperity. Governments (with less resources) take note and play enabling role to foster growth through entrepreneurship	"Hacking" seen as a means to test and learn to build prototypes that can become real businesses.	Patient Investors and tech savvy angel investors get their hands dirty and invest in potential, not just quick payback deals.
	New models of capitalism from homegrown "AfriCapitalism" to social venture/impact investing point to being able to serve the "bottom of the pyramid at scale".	Returning Diaspora talent or expats help build up ecosystem with relevant skills, networks and investment capital or remittance channel support. Global talent from leading universities such as Stanford, Harvard and MIT engage in Africa helping transfer knowledge and skills.	Success stories and development of Exits for investors bring in "laggard investors".
	Technology seen as a key catalyst to reduce cost and enable innovation.		Multinationals recognize and invest in regional R&D offices not just sales or cheap outsourcing hubs.

Table 2: Africa Tech Blueprint in Summary

References:

Rise of the Global Entrepreneurial Class, Scott Hartley, http://www.forbes.com/sites/scotthartley/2012/03/25/conspicuous_creation/

BongoHive maps tech incubators in Africa, Olivia Solon, http://www.wired.co.uk/news/archive/2012-02/23/bongohive-maps-tech-incubators

Tony Elumelu Foundation, http://www.tonyelumelufoundation.org/

Meltwater Entrepreneurial School of Technology, http://www.meltwater.org/

PayPal Mafia, Wikipedia, http://en.wikipedia.org/wiki/PayPal_Mafia

The Lean Startup, Eric Ries, http://theleanstartup.com/

African Innovations, The Stream: AlJazeera, http://stream.aljazeera.com/episode/22129

Dead Aid, Dr. Dambisa Moyo, http://www.dambisamoyo.com/books-and-publications/book/dead-aid

Disruptive Innovation in the African Tech Context

By Will Mutua

What is it really to disrupt, or what is a disruptive innovation? And to put it in the African context, what does 'disruption' mean for the continent and what are the distribution opportunities?

Disruptive Innovation is NOT making a good product better

Clayton Christensen, the Harvard Business School professor who coined the term and came up with the theory of disruptive innovation describes it as that kind of innovation that transforms a product that was traditionally complex and expensive to being widely accessible & affordable. The easiest example of this is the PC revolution and how companies like Apple and Microsoft undercut the giants of the computing world by introducing these much lower cost, much simpler to use computers as opposed to the traditional mainframes that were way too expensive, even for many companies.

Disruptive Innovation is about New Markets

A truly disruptive innovation will be targeted at an entirely new market spectrum. Disruptive innovation is not about building '*better products for our best customers*' but really it's about creating totally new products (or a new class of an existing product) for totally new customers. Using the PC revolution example, Apple and Microsoft literally created a market for the Personal Computer. An interesting concept here is that of "*competing against non-consumption*", that is, creating products that are not really competing against another product but competing to get non-consumers to start using that product.

Disruptive Innovation in Africa

Given this idea of competing against non-consumption, it could be that Africa might be a great place for disruptive innovation. The gap between rich and poor is generally quite high, and the proportion of the lower income population is higher than the middle-income populace.

This means that there are fewer people who are able to enjoy certain things in life simply because of the purchasing power they have. Often-times, the people in the lower income population would like to enjoy the same things as those in the middle class but cannot, and there you have a non-consuming market for which one can disrupt to take advantage of.

Framing this theory in the African context, what's a great example of disruption in action? And what opportunities are there for entrepreneurs to create disruption?

Case: Mobile Money Disrupted Traditional Banking

Five years ago, Kenya's dominant Mobile Network Operator, Safaricom, introduced a new product offering – MPESA. Five years later and multiple awards later, MPESA is the definitive case for the transformative potential of mobile money.

MPESA was really a disruptive technology. Who was disrupted? – The banks, the traditional financial institutions. MPESA (and really mobile money in general) represents this concept of competing against non-consumption. The core tenet of mobile money has come to be stated in the goal of "banking the *unbanked*". Basically, people who have no access to or no capacity to qualify for a traditional bank account – non-consumers.

The big question now is, who's going to disrupt Safaricom in Kenya?

Perhaps that disruptor in the mobile money space could be found in a much smaller mobile money network that boasts a modest 70,000 subscribers versus Safaricom's 15.21 million customers, and moved Sh. 1.13 billion in December 2011 versus Safaricom's 116.6 billion.

That's Mobi Pay's Tangaza platform.

While their figures seem modest, they've overtaken even the second largest MNO in Kenya, Airtel Money, which has a larger subscriber base of about 3.16 million but moved only KES 420 million in December 2011, less than half of Tangaza's volumes. In fact, Tangaza has the lowest number of subscribers.

A key differentiator of the Tangaza offering is that they support cross-network transactions, something that the MNOs have been reluctant to embrace.

Opportunity to disrupt: Energy

Much of Africa's population is rural, with much of the rural population having very limited or no access to electricity. It is estimated actually that very soon, more of Africa's population will have access to mobile telephony but not electricity. This presents a great opportunity to exploit the concept of competing against non-consumption.

The thing with clean energy such as solar is that the technology is still quite expensive and would be out of reach for rural Africa. It is interesting, however, that there are amazing innovations that will open up this low-income segment. One case of a company's that's poised to create disruption is Egg-Energy in Tanzania.

EGG-energy

EGG-energy is a Tanzanian company that calls itself the *"Netflix of batteries"*. EGG aims at helping low-income consumers in Sub-Saharan Africa gain access to clean, affordable energy, using a unique strategy based around portable rechargeable batteries. Their business is based on the fact that 80% of the Tanzanian population live within five kilometers of a transmission line and less than 15% having access to electricity – that is the non-consuming market for electricity in Tanzania. Could they disrupt Tanzania's power companies in the long run?

Opportunity to disrupt: Smartphones

One of the most evident opportunities for disruption in Africa is in the handset manufacturing industry. It has been predicted that Smartphones will become cheaper as more and more higher end features also appear on devices in the lower end of the spectrum.

Huawei made a killing in Kenya with its $100 IDEOS Smartphone, and already the prediction is that the cost of Smartphones will go down to close to $50. According to Vodacom CEO, Pieter Uys, in an interview with Memeburn:

"We've now broken the US$100 barrier for a smartphone. In 18 months' time that US$100 will be US$50... if not less. And then it keeps coming down — that's what happened with 'normal' phones."

In conclusion, there are many kinds of products and services that have non-consuming markets in Africa – not just in technology but other sectors as well. This makes the continent a ripe destination for disruptive innovations.

References:

A conversation with professor Clayton Christensen, Charlie Rose, http://www.charlierose.com/view/interview/1573

Tangaza Mobile Money Service, http://www.tangaza321.com/

M-Pesa tightens grip on Sh1.2 trillion mobile money market, David Mugwe and Okuttah Mark, http://mobilemoneyafrica.com/m-pesa-tightens-grip-on-sh1-2-trillion-mobile-money-market/

EGG Energy Tanzania, http://egg-energy.com/

A geek at the helm: Memeburn's interview with Vodacom CEO Pieter Uys, Matthew Buckland, http://memeburn.com/2012/03/a-geek-at-the-helm-vodacom-ceo-speaks-to-memeburn/

7 steps to raising Seed Investment for Africa focused Tech Startups

By Mbwana Alliy

As various countries in Africa position themselves as tech hubs on the continent, more and more entrepreneurs are trying to raise seed investments for tech startups. However, raising seed funding is hard enough for start-ups in other markets, it's probably at least twice as hard in Africa, even though Africa is uniquely positioned and there is rising curiosity and recognition of real growth investment opportunities outside of the BRIC countries.

Below is a list of pointers for those trying to raise seed financing. While the points are generic and could apply to really anyone in any other market who's trying to raise financing for their startup, some tips that are tailored for the African or Africa-based startup - "Reality of Africa", follow each point. Hopefully, this helps start-ups navigate a difficult but necessary process if we are to see more entrepreneurial activity and to grow the ecosystem in Africa.

1. Make sure you are ready – Checklist

Why exactly are you seeking funding in the first place? Can you identify with great detail and specificity what kind of funding you are seeking and for what purpose you need it?

Entrepreneurs go for financing at different stages; from when they simply have an idea in their head, to startups showing significant progress but are probably stalling and need significant technical/business help and capital infusion to grow their venture. Fundraising also takes a significant amount of time and if the team is small, hitting the road in search of funding might actually harm the business if key individual founders or the CEO spend 6+ months pitching to investors. Hence, it's important to appoint someone in the team to focus on this more (usually the CEO), while freeing up the rest of the team to continue executing.

A poorly prepared startup on the funding road doesn't help either side. A startup with a single founder is disadvantaged vs. a well-rounded team that compliments each other. So it is of vital importance to make sure you have hit key milestones before putting your startup at more risk by spending time on the road searching for funding - you might talk to 50+ potential investors before getting anywhere.

Next, having a product or service out in the marketplace with early customers/users and even revenue is **extremely important**. Investors have many options and they need to see your company gaining traction. With the cost of launching Internet startups dropping everywhere, we will only continue to have more quality startups surface and compete for investors' attention - traction is a real currency. However, being an accomplished entrepreneur and having proven to make investors' money changes the equation – instead of you looking for money, money might be chasing you. Past success is not indicative of future performance, but it certainly helps.

REALITY OF AFRICA

Being ready for seed investment in Africa is definitely different from western markets. It's harder to show revenue for a consumer mobile/Internet start-up; ad networks are just developing, significant scale on internet or mobile users is harder to achieve, and payment ecosystems and trust on the Internet (different on mobile) is not mature - but this is fast changing. On the enterprise buyer side, most don't understand technology that much to decide between different offerings. However, if a technology solution solves a unique problem and gets adopted by a mainstream customer, being first to market has a huge advantage.

From observation, many African startup founders also downplay their previous success too much, if you ran a successful tech development firm for many years, talk up the experience, it shows that you have what it takes to recruit local staff and build a business. If raising money from Silicon Valley, traction for Africa startups has to be very high to generate interest and compete against what other options angel investors have and because of the unfamiliarity of the market at this stage. A particularly difficult situation is not being able to bootstrap to show enough traction, this could be because the founders don't have enough resources to get their idea off the ground and get some initial traction or because of the kind of startup; for example, it's hard to do an energy/clean tech startup without raising significant capital vs. a mobile/web internet startup.

2. Create a clean and short deck, plus list your startup on Angel List, VC4Africa and other such online investor communities/networks - but this is

no substitute for business planning, deep analysis and connecting face to face with potential Investors

A great deck not only communicates the problem and solution, it also creates an emotional connection and inspires whoever is looking at it to want to learn more. The deck is often e-mailed to investors, they take a 5-minute look and then they decide whether to follow up and learn more. Treat the deck as just that, a deck; it's not a full business plan. Here are some more guidelines:

- Don't put too many figures/statistics – limit to 3 per slide - be selective of the most important ones

- Use strong visuals showing the product and screenshots of the service in action

- Focus on the team, achievements and why you are unique to address this problem.

- Make sure the deck flows and tells a story about how you came across the problem, who you are and how you are best positioned to provide the solution

- Limit it to no more than 10-12 slides, the shorter, the better. Other supporting data can be put in an Appendix.

It's more difficult than one may think, to create a great deck with the requirements above; it's a continuous process whilst getting feedback. Knowing your audience is imperative. Getting a designer to polish up the deck may even be needed. A 1-2 page brief may also be a good idea. In addition, don't be afraid to be creative and show off relevant skills, if you have a HTML5 designer on the team for instance, why not use that skill to create something slick and fancy? (Here's a nice example: 1. http://investors.dressrush.com/)

Next, leverage online investor communities such as AngelList, the *"LinkedIn for Startups"*. Although currently dominated by Silicon Valley startups and angel investors, it could be used internationally if both startups and investors abroad use it. At the moment, it could be useful if you are targeting Silicon Valley investors. Angel List provides some great features for your startup such as newsfeed notifications of progress in your startup, you can put advisors, early investors etc… In short it becomes a place where investors can discover and track your progress.

There are other such online communities and networks specifically targeted at the African startup: VC4Africa and Human IPO are some examples.

However, you should also be sure to have a solid business analysis behind your startup and industry. When investors dig deeper in a 2nd or 3rd meeting they'll ask for this. It is critical to show that you've done your homework rather than dismissing the questions as irrelevant. However, if investors persistently ask for data that doesn't exist or impossible to predict at the level of an early stage startup, it could be a sign that they are just looking for an excuse to say no as part of their "due diligence process" or just don't get technology in Africa.

REALITY OF AFRICA

The deck for an African start-up needs to focus heavily on the problem being solved and traction (users or revenue) that the business has achieved, more so than would be the case for those in western markets. Given that cutting edge engineering skills are often lacking in Africa, highlighting the development team's previous programming accomplishments will go a long way to ensure that the product risk is minimal. Good design is also a big differentiator.

If you can show a good and complementing mix of local and foreign talent, especially for a business with significant on-the-ground presence would be an added advantage. For example, can anyone on the team speak fluent Swahili when operating in Tanzania and trying to address the bottom of the pyramid market?

Also note that a deck targeted at social impact investors will look very different from one targeted at traditional investors in terms of content and what is important. This leads to the next point - what sorts of investors are ideal for your venture? But first, a word on analysis: focus on key assumptions: why did you choose Kenya over Nigeria or South Africa? Does Africa really need another mobile money solution and what problem are you really trying to solve? Will people really find and download your application? There is a lot of data on the growth of Africa tech these days, how do these numbers support your startup?

Be sure to outline how the funding you are seeking to raise will help you achieve your next set of goals (something often overlooked). Will this get you to revenue, scale, launch a new product or are you just topping off funding because you are out of money to fund operations?

3. Identify a short list of relevant investors - key criteria for Africa.

Startups can waste lot of time pitching to the wrong investor audience. At the same time, you never know whether an investor is interested in your space or not. It's a time management balance, so it's wise to give careful thought to whom you may want to target. Start with your closest connections, and then proceed from there. Don't forget to include friends and family in this since they know your character best and can provide moral support.

Some key considerations:

- Do they have the capacity to provide the level of financing you need AND a connection or interest in your kind of company?

- Do they understand technology and the nature of tech startups e.g. the delicate balance between growth and profitability?

- Do they provide value-add knowledge, networks and mentoring? What is their expertise?

- Do they treat their investment like putting money in the bank and receiving interest, or is it a risky bet at the casino through which they learn and have fun? Is this a "feel good" or an "impact investment"? - Make sure you line up accordingly. Sometimes their investment is just a way for them to "learn about the space".

- Are they investing for a small stake in a big pie, or big stake in a small pie?

- Do they have the bandwidth to assist you, based on other investments and their day job? Remember a savvy angel investor has many options and some like to get really involved, others are more hands off. Are you the best option right now and why?

REALITY OF AFRICA

The reality, at least for the moment, is that there just aren't many active angel investors in Africa who understand technology, start-ups and who meet this list's criteria. There also aren't enough rich uncles in Africa to go around and support all entrepreneurial endeavors of friends and families (but this is slowly changing as success stories realize they can give back to the ecosystem and also make money). Even then, not many investors are accessible or even know how to angel invest. Significant networking assistance is needed to reach them and get above the noise. African Diaspora living abroad have significant capital that they could mobilize for your venture - there are many Kenyans, Nigerians, South Africans etc. living abroad who might be looking to invest back home. The Indus Entrepreneurs (TIE) network of Indian Diaspora, for example, has links to Silicon Valley that include tons of angel investors that might comprise the Indian population residing in East Africa. They might be eyeing Africa as an attractive investment in technology, especially if India is becoming increasingly competitive, saturated or too corrupt and bureaucratic. In Silicon Valley, a connection to The African Network (TAN) might also be able of help. The

Middle East is another option - UAE, Oman are heavy investors in East Africa for instance.

A word on impact investors: they started in microfinance where they realized that one could profitably serve the poor in India, Bangladesh, Latin America and Africa, and have now moved into other areas (health, education etc…). It's a new industry and as a result many change their investment strategy as much as the wind in the Sahara or the Indian Ocean changes direction! Some are more stable than others - one can tell how stable they are by looking at their investment portfolio. Impact investors are also less likely to ask about high financial returns and exit options as they mainly care about what "impact" you are making- such as number of jobs created, reduction of malaria prevalence, serving an under-served population etc…

4. Network and Educate Investors

Ask for advice and you might get money. Update progress on Angel List. Draft and test your e-mail pitches, find investors at conferences, use your social skills well, how you interact and reach investors is a key skill. It's like dating… It also communicates what you might be like to work with. The most networked people do better in business than just being smart and savvy. This is twice as important when it comes to getting angel investment, it is about whom you know and who can refer and vouch for you.

STOP! Before you proceed, go through points 1 - 3 a few times. The fourth point becomes the point at which you start talking to people and work your way to investors. You'll be repeating steps 1-3 over and over for further funding rounds. No shortcuts. Learn to do it once because you'll be doing it again!

REALITY OF AFRICA

Africa needs tons of education for foreign investors due to preconceived notions of Africa despite growing interest. As a result, they might be risk-averse right now, till they get more familiar with the continent. Try to avoid the "drive-by investors" who might not add much value apart from their money. For local investors, it means focusing on how the technology works. Even after foreign investors "get Africa" it's really difficult for them to anchor themselves her needs since they are not living and breathing the problem you are trying to solve -they might even need come to Africa to see the problem you are trying to solve first-hand. This means increasing the time it takes to raise money from foreign investors. European investors might take less time to educate versus American investors but they might not get the technology aspects as much as a Silicon Valley investor. Also, their risk appetite and familiarity with tech angel investing is likely to be different.

An ideal investor would have some foreign expertise that brings tech and management discipline/experience and a local partner who can provide local context and connections.

5. Practice the pitch and work up to your ideal investor(s)

Know the toughest questions upfront and address them intelligently and honestly. You might have to go through "Gatekeepers" who have the connection to the high profile investor, understand their position; don't assume they will just make an e-mail intro out of the blue. Treat them well; their job is not to refer every start-up. That defies the point of a gatekeeper. Note the common questions (most are not primarily interested in the technical aspects such as whether the product is built in PHP or Ruby!). Sometimes you'll get questions to which there simply are no good answers, don't be afraid to say "I don't know", it's a mark of maturity, but be sure to convey that you will find out or are actively working to solve that problem and you are a fast learner.

REALITY OF AFRICA

For entrepreneurs originating from Africa, the pitch delivery needs to be practiced to perfection. Being able to pitch in 6-10 minutes is daunting for most entrepreneurs, but it should be an opportunity to distill your startup into the key elements. In Silicon Valley, you never know when you might have to talk about your startup, could be at a conference, in a bar or an elevator (hence the elevator pitch!), so most startup founders can talk about their startups really succinctly.

If you have to talk too long - see point 4 on education. You might need to follow up or prepare with the person introducing /"referring" you to the investor. Here is a checklist of questions you should anticipate and prepare good answers for:

- Africa is the 'dark continent'; it's unstable, right?

- Do Africans have real money to spend?

- There is serious currency risk, check out the inflation rates in Kenya and Uganda, for instance. How will your business handle it?

- Nigeria is the best place to do a start-up right? It's a big market! Why are you in Tanzania?

- Can you hire the technical and managerial talent to grow your venture?

- How will I get my money back via Exit?

6. Scoring an anchor and influential investor can significantly boost your chances

But be careful who this is! Refer to **point 3**. Accelerators and incubators can act as a *"stamp of approval"* and also make it efficient for investors coming to visit a region in Africa. In Silicon Valley, getting vouched and having influential personalities such as Ron Conway or Dave McClure on your side can get you a long way to closing your funding round. AngelList once more presents a very efficient way of accomplishing this but it is no substitute for face-to-face interaction if you can get it. Sometimes you are better off preparing really well and scoring an introduction from someone influential than trying to talk to a mass of investors who don't understand you (at least at the beginning).

REALITY OF AFRICA

Incubators and Accelerators popping up in Africa are helping to solve this. Accelerators like the Umbono in South Africa or Meltwater in Ghana can be a fast track to get to this step. It might take you 6 months to get to this step on your own or 3 months if your join the "right accelerator". Be sure to evaluate them properly, the founders can have significant connections to real tech investors - who is the Ron Conway of Africa? The person might exist, but they might not be as publicly visible as the Silicon Valley equivalent. Try get yourself into regional pitch contests in Africa such as Pivot East in Kenya, for instance, that is organized by the iHub and sponsored by many other startup-friendly organizations that provide proven regional and global visibility.

7. Be wary of terms and make sure you have a clean cap table

But don't overly negotiate. You are getting married, but it's one of many spouses on the long road to success. Term sheets for startups are becoming increasingly standardized across the world. Some VCs are even providing their standard documents on their website that you can customize.

REALITY OF AFRICA

African investors not familiar with start-up term sheets and a country's legal framework around concepts such as employee stock pools (setting aside shares in your company to motivate new employees with success in the company) and convertible notes (a hybrid debt/equity investment instrument common in early stage start-up); they could harm a start-up by demanding unreasonable terms and not ensuring the risk and reward of the start-up team and investors are adequately balanced. This can kill a start-up. The big advice here is to find a lawyer who understands both sides and can educate appropriately. Do your research.

Finally, remember the old investment cliché: *"we invest in people, not ideas"*, it's actually true. Treat your angel/seed investor the same.

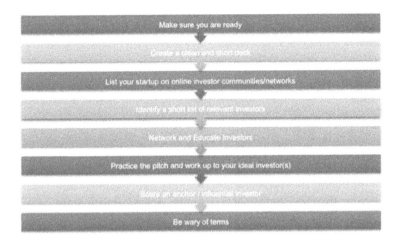

Figure 9: Summary: Raising Seed Funding for your (Africa/Africa-based) Startup

References:

Angel List, http://www.angel.co/

Should Startups Focus on Profitability or Not, Mark Suster, http://www.bothsidesofthetable.com/2011/12/27/should-startups-focus-on-profitability-or-not/

TiE Silicon Valley, http://sv.tie.org/

The African Network, http://www.theafricannetwork.org/

Mobile Banking Takes off in Nigeria,
http://www.gsb.stanford.edu/news/headlines/oviosu_mobil
e_2012.html?cmpid=twitter

AfriLabs, http://afrilabs.com/

Umbono,
http://www.google.co.za/intl/en/umbono/index.html

Meltwater Entrepreneurial School of Technology,
http://www.meltwater.org/

Pivot East, http://pivoteast.com/

Employee Stock Ownership Plans,
http://www.quora.com/Employee-Stock-Ownership-
Plans?q=employee+stock

Convertible Note, http://www.quora.com/Convertible-
Notes?q=convertibe+note

HumanIPO, http://www.humanipo.com/

VC4Africa, http://vc4africa.biz/

Mending Africa's Tech Skills Gap & Tapping into its Youthful Population to Power Innovation in Tech

By Will Mutua

"In a rapidly changing technology world, it's not only important that one understands how to do your current job/technology well, but also be exposed to new ones, particularly in open source, cloud computing and mobile development technologies that may not have originated from the enterprise segment or the 10 year old technology used by your bank." – Mbwana Alliy

Africa's youthful population is where it's at!

According to the Youth Division of the African Union Commission, about 65% of Africa's total population is below the age of 35 years, and over 35% are between the ages of 15 and 35, making Africa the most youthful continent. By 2020, it is projected that out of 4 people, 3 will be on average 20 years old. About 10 million young African youth enter the labor market each year.

According to an International Labor Organization (ILO) report (see references section), a majority of Africa's population is under 30 years of age, (two thirds being under 25 according to the Africa Commission) and the median age is just 18 years. Youth unemployment in Sub-Saharan Africa is twice that of adults (12.8 for youth and 6.5 for adults) and triples that of adults in the case of North Africa (27.1 percent for youth and 7 percent for adults).

Approached in the right manner, the youth bulge in Africa presents an unprecedented potential market for those who can understand this demographic and provide what they demand; a massive potential in skilled and unskilled labor force that can truly transform the continent. According to the Africa Commission, youth will account for almost 30% of the total African labor force by 2015. If appropriately skilled and exposed, this youthful population can easily provide the brains and smarts to power Africa's rise particularly as far as technology and innovation go.

Douglas Cohen, in an article titled "*The IT Skills Gap is Everyone's Business*" (see references), explains the ICT skills gap in South Africa:

"There is a shortage of ICT skills in the South African market. That is a fact. There is however a difference of

opinion on the scale of shortage. The National Department of Labour last issued a National Master Scarce Skills list in April 2008, indicating the ICT sector needed a minimum of 37,565 IT professionals to ensure adequate skills in this sector. However, the results of a more recent ICT survey, conducted by IT Web and the Jo'burg Centre for Software has found the department underestimated, by almost half, how many ICT skills are needed in SA. The suggestion therefore is that the 'real' skills shortage can be as high as 70,000 practitioners – more than 25% of the current workforce."

The World Bank *Knowledge Economy Indicator (KEI)* comprises innovation, education and ICT scores, measuring a region's innovativeness against these. Generally speaking, Africa lags behind other regions on the indicator. But even more important is the evident relation between education and innovation. Regions with better scores on education tend to be more innovative.

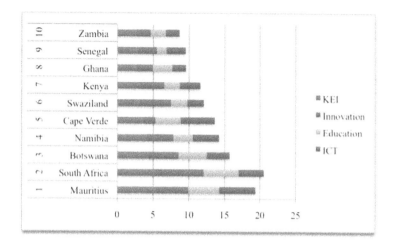

Figure 10: World Bank Knowledge Economy Indicator – Top 10 in Africa, Data Source:
http://info.worldbank.org/etools/kam2/KAM_page5.asp

Crippling Tech Curricula

Most institutions of higher learning in Africa have static tech curricula, as compared to the dynamism of the real world of technology. Most students are stuck at the level of outdated, obsolete concepts (across the open source and proprietary spectrum) that put them at a disadvantage upon graduation. Many tech firms have to re-train fresh graduates upon hiring them so that they can come up to speed with the realities of technology in the real world.

Industry – Business Gap

The tech curricula problem is aggravated all the more by the gap between industry and the academic world. The problem is simple, ICT-related businesses operate in the 'real world' of technology that is highly dynamic. To be competitive, they have to constantly be on the lookout for what's new, rapidly adapting as things change – when new technologies come up, when the major tech companies such as Google and Microsoft take strategic routes that set the pace for what direction technology will take in future... The most successful ICT companies have to be agile.

On the other hand, the academic world is sort of closed up in a cocoon where the industry's dynamism does not affect curricula. The same things are taught year in, year out, with little or no change to reflect the tech world reality. Unless a student is exposed elsewhere, or they happen to be really curious, they're stuck. To make matters worse, the education system often trains students to *not* be inquisitive and explorative.

In Kenya, for example, many have complained against the 8-4-4 curriculum, saying that it's basically a system that encourages cramming and regurgitating. The fact of the matter is that even before they get to university, students have already been accustomed to receiving without question what the teacher gives them, then getting an exam in which all they have to do is give back to the teacher exactly what the teacher gave them in the exact same way, else they fail.

Speaking at a conference on e-Learning in Eastern Africa, Mr. Mike Macharia, CEO of Seven Seas Technologies, a Kenya-based regional ICT services provider notes:

" ... There' s an urgent need to incorporate industry needs in university curricula across all our universities to ensure industry relevance.

Time has come for all the stakeholders in the higher education sector to join hands and tackle the skills deficiency problem to avoid sending out to the job market graduates trained under IT environments, who are not aligned to the dynamic ICT Industry. It is costly to have fresh graduates, hired as engineers on the bench and not billable for several months before we can actively deploy them to customer environments, a practice quite the opposite in the accounting industry."

Solutions

What are possible solutions to the IT skills gap dilemma? Altering university curricula is a long process; you can't just wake up tomorrow and say, "Hey, let's drop this and start teaching that." and just do it. Are there other alternatives? Is there anything that's currently providing a solution?

1. Tech hubs

Tech hubs across Africa are providing brilliant learning spaces outside the confines of strict curricula. Before tech hubs, it was difficult for students to get direct access to and interact with industry practitioners. Meetups and tech talks in these community environments provide great opportunities for students' exposure. With this exposure, the students can then take the initiative to go out and learn for themselves.

2. Industry Steps In

It may not be the core business of industry practitioners to provide training to young students, but it is to their advantage to have the necessary skills readily available. This is what must have led the likes of Seven Seas Technologies to invest in training freshly graduated university students. The alternative, importing the necessary skills, is a costly affair. Perhaps more companies should step in to fill this gap in like manner; at the end of the day, it is to the benefit of the organization and the ecosystem at large.

3. Diaspora & Third party initiatives

One of the best examples is Coders4Africa:

*"Coders4Africa was created in 2010 through the efforts of five friends who collectively have over 40 years of experience in the software engineering and development field. We are a not-for-profit organization with an initiative that focuses on providing professional training and certification on a variety of platforms to 1,000 African software and application developers by the year 2016. After years of interaction with technologists in Africa, we decided to focus on software development as a way of giving back to the communities we originated from. Being born and raised in Africa, although educated in the United States, gave us an advantage in regards to bridging the gap between Africans and the diaspora." - **Kwame Andah (Co-Founder, Coders4Africa)***

Such initiatives underscore the critical role that the diaspora can play in terms of knowledge transfer. Those who have had the opportunity to study and work off the continent, gaining valuable, world-class skills can engage in transferring those skills back home.

At the end of the day however, *innovation is not just a matter of having raw skills*. It's about applying those raw skills ingeniously. It's about thinking outside the box and applying the necessary skills to create.

The beauty about tech skills, especially when it comes to programming, is that the individual can acquire these skills fairly easily. The World Wide Web harbors a wealth of great learning material that is free to use, plus the necessary tools are also available for free download. Several great influencers and innovators in technology were not even schooled in tech but were self-taught.

As we noted, Africa's youth are tech-savvy, eager to learn, agile and have a great desire to carve out for themselves a better future, free of the stain of the continent's misconceptions. Rightly skilled, this young population can be the engine to drive Africa forward into its future. Jon Kalan, writing for the Huffington Post notes regarding Nairobi's youth:

"The country's slowly improving education system is churning out a new generation of university graduates who are aggressive, ambitious, and hungry for a better future. They are fiercely proud of Nairobi, and feel they hold the responsibility for its economic future and its emergence in the global spotlight in their hands. They no longer graduate university with hopes of ending up at the once best paying jobs in town — UN agencies and the scores of other well-financed NGOs. Instead they dream of starting their own business, or finding work in an increasingly robust private sector full of entrepreneurial ideas."

References:

United Nations Population Division, http://www.un.org/esa/population/unpop.htm

Africa Youth Report 2011, UNECA, http://www.uneca.org/ayr2011/African%20Youth%20Report_2011_Final.pdf

Africa: How the Development of Youth Can Contribute Towards Poverty Alleviation, Archbishop Njongo Ndugane, http://allafrica.com/stories/201009140109.html

Youth Bulge: A Demographic Dividend or a Demographic Bomb in Developing Countries?, Justin Yifu Lin, http://blogs.worldbank.org/developmenttalk/youth-bulge-a-demographic-dividend-or-a-demographic-bomb-in-developing-countries

Regional Overview Youth in Africa, UN, http://social.un.org/youthyear/docs/Regional%20Overview%20Youth%20in%20Africa.pdf

Africa's Growing Youth Population - Ronak Gopaldas, ABNDigital, http://www.youtube.com/watch?v=bzBqh09xb88

Africa's Position on Youth, http://africa-youth.org/files/africa_position.html

Africa's Response to the Youth Unemployment Crisis: Regional Report, International Labour Organization (ILO), http://www.ilo.org/wcmsp5/groups/public/---africa/documents/publication/wcms_184325.pdf

Kenya Julisha ICT Report: Invest in New Skills, Mbwana Alliy, http://afrinnovator.com/blog/2011/11/24/kenya-julisha-ict-report-invest-in-new-skills-its-called-human-capital/

The IT Skills Gap is Everyone's Business, Douglas Cohen, http://www.idgconnect.com/blog-abstract/429/douglas-cohen-south-africa-the-it-skills-gap-everyone-business-part

Joburg Center for Software Engineering, http://www.jcse.org.za/

World Bank Knowledge Assessment Methodology, http://worldbank.com/kam

Seven Seas Technology, http://www.sevenseastech.com/

Seven Seas Technologies to bridge ICT skills gap, BizTech Africa, http://www.biztechafrica.com/article/seven-seas-technologies-bridge-ict-skills-gap/352/?section=business

Coders4Africa, http://coders4africa.org/

Interview with Coders4Africa Founders, Will Mutua, http://afrinnovator.com/blog/2011/04/01/interview-with-coders4africa-founders/

Potential, Poverty, Politics & Parties: Why Kenya Attracts America's Best & Brightest Young Social Entrepreneurs, Jonathan Kalan, http://www.huffingtonpost.com/jonathan-kalan/potential-poverty-politic_b_969338.html

Nurturing the Innovative Nature in Africa through Education

By Will Mutua

Globally, the discussion around innovation has been one of great interest especially in the wake of troubling economic times in the recent past. The discussion is strong in relation to Africa's situation as well.

Innovation sometimes can be a bit hard to describe in exact terms but one thing is for sure, you always know genuine innovation or innovativeness when you see it. Yet, it is a critical component to our ability to deal with the challenges of today and the future, the world over.

If this is true, then societies or nations that manage to bake in a culture of innovation into their social fabric will, in a sense, be more insured against the uncertainties of the future than those that do not.

The *World Economic Forum Global Competitiveness Report 2011 – 2012* conducted a study of the competitiveness of 142 economies around the world and identified innovation as one of 12 pillars of competitiveness: Institutions, Infrastructure,

Macroeconomic environment, Health and primary
education, Higher education and training, Goods market
efficiency, Labor market efficiency, Financial market
development, Technological readiness, Market size,
Business sophistication and *Innovation*, as well as3 stages
of economic development:

1. **Factor-driven economies**: Compete primarily on
   the basis of natural resources and unskilled labor.

2. **Efficiency-driven economies**: Where the key is to
   create efficiencies in the production processes.

3. **Innovation-driven economies**: Compete on
   differentiated and sophisticated products and
   production processes.

Most Sub-Saharan African states, according to the research,
fall within the first stage, where the economy is primarily
driven by exploitation of natural resources. In today's
world, it is imperative to create a differentiated and
sophisticated economy in order to truly be competitive. So
for African states to become significant players in the
global economy, ways to move up the ladder to innovation-
driven economies ought to be established.

But how does Africa stack up against the rest of the world innovation wise? The international graduate business school and research institution, INSEAD, in collaboration with the World Intellectual Property Organization (WIPO), produces a *Global Innovation Index* (GII) that aims at giving quantifiable answers to this question. According to the 2011 report that studied the innovativeness of 125 countries, African states don't stack up very well against much of the rest of the world: Mauritius and South Africa are the highest ranked African countries (53 and 59 respectively). Tunisia, Ghana, Namibia, Botswana, Egypt, Kenya, Morocco, Nigeria, Senegal, Swaziland, Cameroun, Tanzania, Uganda, Mali, Malawi, Rwanda, Madagascar, Zambia, Cote d'Ivoire, Benin, Zimbabwe, Burkina Faso, Ethiopia, Niger, Sudan and Algeria rank between 64 and 125. The BRIC countries (Brazil, Russia, India and China) rank 47, 56, 62 and 29 respectively. The most recent GII (2012) shows there's some reason to be optimistic – Mauritius still leads the index in the Sub-Saharan region, this year ranking 49th overall, up 5 places from their ranking in 2011. South Africa has also moved up from 59th to 54th.

The top 10 African countries in the 2012 report are as follows:

Country	SS-Africa Rank 2012	Overall Rank 2012	Overall Rank 2011
Mauritius	1	49	53
South Africa	2	54	59
Namibia	3	73	78
Swaziland	4	82	101
Botswana	5	85	79
Ghana	6	92	70
Kenya	7	96	89
Senegal	8	97	100
Rwanda	9	102	109
Gabon	10	106	-

Table 3: Global Innovation Index 2012 Ranking Top 10 Africa

So how do you peg down innovation and bake it into the very fabric of a society so that innovating is a normal occurrence versus one that takes considerable effort to bring about, especially in the African context?

A Nature that needs to be nurtured

Innovation comes naturally to humans. One thing is for sure, human beings have a knack for surviving against all odds and that's the reason why we're still here and many specific peoples have not been completely wiped off the face of the earth by some major catastrophe or challenge in their history. Innovation has played a big role in mankind's 'stickability' – his adapting to the many changes the planet has experienced historically in order to survive.

Despite it being a *natural* capacity, one thing is for sure: in many cases *innovation needs to be nurtured*. The *naturalness* comes forth quite clearly in the face of an immediate threat, for example, or an urgent need or problem that needs to be solved. As they say, 'necessity is the mother of invention'. People will find the most innovative, inventive and ingenious means to get out of a threatening situation or to solve some urgent problem. If you've watched the movie '127 hours', you'll have a clear idea of just how far a human being will go to find a means of surviving the worst of circumstances or to solve some dire problem (*cutting off one's arm may not quite count as innovation but you get the point*).

So part of our innovative, creative capacity comes from, or at least is brought out by our survival instinct.

The question then arises, *how do you bring out this amazing human capability without an immediate threat to survival or immediate challenge?* It's a valid question because if we're touting innovation as the answer to future challenges, we have to find a means to bring out that innovative capacity to bear *before* those challenges become an immediate matter of concern.

It starts early

If you haven't watched any of Sir Ken Robinson's TED Talks (see references) you simply must! Sir Robinson, in his uniquely humorous way, explains how we get '*educated out of creativity*'. The premise is that we're all born with a great natural capacity for creativity and innovation (you just need to watch a toddler long enough to draw the same conclusion), but as we grow up that nature is slowly corroded away especially by our interactions with the education systems we're put through.

Sadly, the state of most public education systems validates Sir Robinson's concerns. The education system in most African countries is typically designed *against* the ability to bring out and nurture the student's capacity for innovation and creativity. In fact, it does a good job at accomplishing the opposite – squashing almost every iota of creative capacity in the student. Why is this so? Perhaps because the system was set up in a time when 'innovation' was not a buzzword or a critical consideration of what it would take for an individual and nation to navigate the changes of a globalized world.

Education and a culture of innovation

A culture of innovation has to be supported by the right kind of education for the members of that society. Why?

Simply put, you can't educate one way and then ask the student to act in the opposite way.

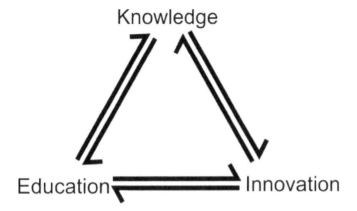

Figure 11: The Knowledge Triangle

If we have an education system that kills the creativity, innovativeness and inventiveness of students, why would we expect those same students who in future would be in charge of our society and running our economies, to turn around into something they were not educated for? The result is an *anti-innovation culture.* It certainly is not impossible, but it sure would be hard to alter years of learned traits. It's hard to change someone's way of thinking when all their student life, which normally would account for close to a quarter or more of one's life, they were taught to cram and regurgitate.

Most students emerging from most of our education systems have *static knowledge* – what they were taught by the teacher in class and what they were asked for in their examinations. *To foster a culture of innovation, we need to produce students who don't just receive and store information in their brains, but those who create new knowledge – dynamic knowledge - based on what they've learnt.*

The Knowledge Triangle (depicted in the diagram above) shows the linkages between education, knowledge and innovation. Through education, relevant knowledge is acquired and then applied in innovative ways. Through innovation, new knowledge is created, which can then be passed on through education, creating new opportunities for innovation and so on. *In other words, education is a critical component to innovation and the creation of a knowledge society and knowledge economy.* (See the essay, *"From Factor-Driven to Innovation-Driven Economies in Africa: A Framework for Development of Knowledge Economies"*).

Educating for (or into) the Future

Education has been identified as a key component to the rise of the African continent, and has been a key feature at many forums. In fact, 'Universal Education' is one of the

UN Millennium Development Goals. Many a time, the discussion revolves around *quantity* – getting more students enrolled in schools. However, quality wise, an ill-fitting education for current *and*, more importantly, *future* demands can be almost as bad as no education at all. But what is a quality education in today's times?

In many countries on and off the African continent, educational reform has been a matter of great debate, with many countries embarking on initiatives to reform their education systems. Educational reform is a pretty tough nut to crack for basic reasons, chief amongst which, is dealing with the sheer scale of the system's reach:

- National public education systems are standardized and applicable to the entire population. Where do you start the reform and how do you ensure it permeates through the entire system?

- You have thousands or hundreds of thousands of educators who have been using the status quo for years and decades, before you reach the student you have to deal with the educator in the first place. This could be even harder to do because unlike the students, the teachers are older and have been in the system longer, so a paradigm shift is harder to start and scale.

Based on a simple observation of the world in which we live and that which we will live in the near future, at least four elements should be considered in organizing a relevant system for education:

1. **Creative Experimentation:** The system needs to allow for creative experimentation where students are allowed to apply their creative abilities to existing knowledge to create new knowledge in a practical way.

2. **Entrepreneurship focused**: In the past, the standard progression for students was to go to school, get a degree and you'd be guaranteed a job. In the early years of many African states following their independence, there was a shortage of skilled labor especially for government agencies. Students would be earmarked for well-paying government jobs before graduating; those days are now in the past. The problem nowadays is that there simply aren't enough jobs going around, yet for economic prosperity, the discussion boils down to job creation, which translates to increments in GDP.

The education system has to empower students to be able to create jobs for themselves and others. This ties in with the previous point – creative experimentation ensures students have the capacity to create innovative products, and entrepreneurship skills help students learn how to turn innovative concepts into commercial products and business organizations.

3. **Future focused**: Predicting the future can be a daunting task nowadays, a fact that has been proven by recent occurrences and shifts in economies. All the more why students need to learn skills that prepare them for uncertain and highly dynamic futures. Skills such as adaptability and flexibility need to be core and practical.

4. **Globalized and localized**: Globalization has turned our world upside down and inside out. Occurrences in distant economies create real problems in local ones; at the same time, distant opportunities are accessible locally. Yet, it's critically important for students not to lose their heritage, a component of one's identity.

References:

Can Innovation Drive the Economic Recovery?,
http://techpolicy.com/Blog/May-2011/Can-Innovation-
Drive-the-Economic-Recovery-.aspx

The Global Competitiveness Report 2011-2012, World
Economic Forum,
http://www3.weforum.org/docs/WEF_GCR_Report_2011-
12.pdf

INSEAD, http://www.insead.edu/home/

Global Innovation Index,
http://www.globalinnovationindex.org/

How To Make Africa More Innovative And
Entrepreneurial – Part II – Lessons From The Global
Innovation Index 2011, Brian
LaungAoaehhttp://tekedia.com/44660/africa-innovative-
entrepreneurial-part-ii-lessons-global-innovation-index-
2011/

Sir Ken Robinson, TED,
http://www.ted.com/speakers/sir_ken_robinson.html

UN Millennium Development Goals,
http://www.un.org/millenniumgoals/education.shtml

eLimu Tablet,

http://www.youtube.com/watch?v=3kKd8VnY0-
I&feature=player_embedded

From Factor-Driven to Innovation-Driven Economies in Africa: A Framework for Development of Knowledge Economies

By Will Mutua

According to the *World Economic Forum Competitiveness Report 2011 – 2012,* there are three stages of economic development by which one can classify the world's economies: Factor-driven economies, Efficiency-driven economies and Innovation-driven economies (see the chapter *"Africa and Innovation: Nature and Nurture – Education"* for details about this classification)

The most advanced economies tend to be those in the third stage – innovation-driven economies. These are also economies that have placed a premium on knowledge as a key factor for economic growth; they are 'Knowledge Economies'. In Africa, most nations lag behind as factor-driven economies primarily, based on exploitation of natural resources, which in many cases has not led to sustained and shared economic development because of the so-called 'resource curse'. Only a handful of African economies are efficiency-driven.

In order to be significant player's in the global economy, Africa has to move to the innovation-driven economic level. How?

Leveraging Natural Resources to Build Sophisticated Knowledge Economies

Before getting into the framework, it is worth taking a short detour here to make a comment about the resource-dependence of many African states.

Much as natural resources such as oil and gas have been exploited to the disadvantage of citizens, leading to a situation where the citizens are not benefiting from these resources, the aim should not be to abandon such endeavors altogether. African states should make every effort to find the best and fairest means by which to benefit from their natural resources.

We live in a world where there is a huge demand for natural resources. China, due to its past economic growth, has risen to become a major consumer of natural resources. It's no wonder that China has such a keen interest in Africa. Africa has a lot of what China needs to keep producing and keep growing and consequently China has established itself as Africa's largest trading partner. Standard Bank Group in

2011 projected that China's investment into Africa may rise by 70 percent to $50 billion by 2015 from 2009, as the Asian nation seeks to acquire resources. (Dr. Dambisa Moyo's "Winner Take All" is a good read on this)

The McKinsey Global Institute report on Africa's economies, *"Lions on the move"*, distinguishes four broad categorizations of Africa's economies:

- *Diverse Economies*: Africa's growth engines – Egypt, Tunisia, Morocco, South Africa.

- *Oil Exporters*: Economies that are overly dependent on oil export. They have the highest GDPs but the least diversification. Algeria, Angola and Nigeria being the largest of these.

- *Transition Economies*

- *Pre-transition Economies*

The aim is to create diversified economies; not just diversified, but 'balanced' out.

The Diversified, Balanced Economy

It is pretty clear what a 'diversified' economy is. A diverse and 'balanced' economy is NOT one that places equal importance and equal emphasis to all aspects of a diverse economy. It is, instead:

a) One that places relevant emphasis where it's due, to the measure that it is due.

Perhaps an example will help: There have been several oil finds in a few African countries that previously were not oil producing countries, Kenya, being one of them. What sometimes happens is that the government turns to focus on these 'high-value' natural resources and exploiting them, ignoring other areas. Some nations overspend on oil exploration at the expense of other investments such as education, with an attitude that says, "If we can only strike oil (or some mineral resource) we're sorted!"

To use a metaphor: *What is needed is not to place all your eggs in one basket; or too many eggs in one basket and too few in others; or equal number of eggs in bags of different capacities – but the appropriate number of eggs in the appropriate basket based on the capacity and relative importance of that basket.*

Natural resources, for example, create a limited number of job opportunities; many times the benefits are not shared and there can be devastating complications such as when locals feel they're not benefiting from an oil find in their community. Sole dependence or overdependence on natural resources is not the way to go. Furthermore, what happens when oil reserves start running out? On the other hand, the economic gains from exploiting natural resources can be applied to growing other areas that can create new opportunities for wealth creation, more opportunities for the people and wider distribution of wealth in a sustainable manner.

In other words, leverage one strength to build other parts of the economy. Exploit the oil, it could result in high returns in the short term but realize that the key to relevance in the global economy (now and more so in the future) is in innovation-driven, knowledge-based economics. *Invest more in the present; in what it takes to build such an economy in future* e.g. make significant investments in R&D. Instead of looking for a way out at the time oil reserves start running out, make sure significant investments are being made in building the knowledge economy from the get go – in effect, future-proofing the economy.

b) One that balances economic development with social development, for example, by making sure there's equitable distribution of resources.

A Broad Framework for the Development of the Knowledge Economy

In a Knowledge Economy, *acquisition, creative transformation, sharing and productive application* of knowledge become the key factors for economic development. Let's look at these specific aspects briefly:

1. Acquisition: The society creates efficient processes and mechanisms for the acquisition of relevant, usually highly specialized knowledge from different sources. The acquisition of such knowledge is a sustained effort, leading to the emergence of a high level of expertise in some area of knowledge.

2. Creative Transformation: The society not only acquires knowledge (static knowledge) but creates the means for individuals and organizations (academic, state and corporate) to adapt, refine, 'remix' indigenous knowledge and knowledge from external sources into new forms of knowledge that can be applied to new processes/problems, or existing processes/problems in a more efficient/better way.

3. Sharing: The society allows for the sharing of knowledge so that the processes of acquisition and creative transformation are continuously facilitated while balancing that out with the need for those who create knowledge to benefit (economically) from their efforts (IP). *Knowledge is the economic engine's fuel.*

4. Productive Application: This is the key to transforming a Knowledge *Society* to a Knowledge *Economy*. This is the step that results in the creation of innovative goods and services through entrepreneurship and eventually leads to job creation and increments to GDP.

These four broad aspects of a Knowledge Economy can be matched to four broad factors (pillars) that need to be developed to create a solid foundation and facilitate such an economy.

a) Policy Framework

A policy framework for sharing and benefiting from knowledge is crucial in a knowledge-based economy. The policy framework needs to strike a balance between facilitating free-flow of information and protecting the right to profit from intellectual property. This can be a dicey affair. Sometimes IP can stifle creativity or distract companies when they have to keep fighting one IP lawsuit after another.

In a broader sense, governments also need to create a supporting environment and make relevant investments that support the creation of a Knowledge Economy. A great example here is South Africa. The Department of Science and Technology of South Africa put forth a 10-year plan (2008 – 2018) that seeks to transform the South African economy into a knowledge-based economy. It would appear that their efforts are bearing some fruits so far, given their ranking relative to other African states according to INSEAD's Global Innovation Index.

b) Information and Communications Technologies

ICTs provide the means to codify, store, process and transmit knowledge and information in a fast and efficient (digital) manner.

Significant investments have been made in terms of undersea fiber connectivity between the African continent and the rest of the world. Terrestrial distribution, or the last mile connection, has been a challenge in many cases but those problems will be solved in time. More Africans will have access to broadband as Internet penetration rates continue to rise.

The Nairobi Innovation Hub (iHub) recently embarked on an initiative to build a supercomputer. Such an instrument will be a great asset for the fast processing of data, such as when running scientific experiments, a great tool for R&D. In the process, it will hopefully, also lead to the acquisition of the specialized knowledge it takes to build the supercomputer in the first place. More initiatives of this kind that create the underlying infrastructure, which facilitate a Knowledge Society and Knowledge Economy are needed across the continent.

c) Education & Human Capital Development

In the previous essay, we took a close look at education and its place in the formation of a society in which innovation is the norm; where innovation is baked into the very social fabric of the society. We saw what kinds of considerations need to be factored in to the development of relevant education systems that will support the development of a sustained culture of creativity and innovation; these were:

- Creative Experimentation

- Entrepreneurship focus

- Future focus

- Globalized and localized

Another important aspect as far as education and the creation of knowledge-based economies go is that of *lifelong learning*. In other words, the culture is not one that emphasizes getting an academic qualification and getting a job – but one that supports continuous, *evolutionary* learning – evolutionary, meaning the learning creates new knowledge which is then disseminated through the education system for others to learn, and remix, creating new knowledge continuously.

d) Entrepreneurial Culture

The entrepreneurial culture is the puzzle piece that unlocks productive application of knowledge. Without it, you're basically left with a really good academic system.

It's the entrepreneurs who come across some piece of knowledge, create a link to a real world problem, and figure out how to apply that knowledge to the creation of a product or service that solves the problem in a profitable way, and then go out and bring together all the factors –

capital, labor, organization – that are needed to do this. The entire framework therefore needs to have in-built mechanisms for easy discovery of relevant knowledge, and rapid transformation of knowledge to productive economic activity. As a result jobs are created, productive activity is carried out and GDP grows.

References:

The Global Competitiveness Report 2011-2012, World Economic Forum, http://www3.weforum.org/docs/WEF_GCR_Report_2011-12.pdf

Beijing, a Boon for Africa, Dambisa Moyo, http://www.nytimes.com/2012/06/28/opinion/beijing-a-boon-for-africa.html?_r=3&emc=tnt&tntemail1=y

China's Investment In Africa To Increase To $50 Billion By 2015, Bank Says, Bloomberg News, http://www.bloomberg.com/news/2011-02-22/china-s-investment-in-africa-to-increase-to-50-billion-by-2015-bank-says.html

Winner Takes All, Dambisa Moyo,
http://www.dambisamoyo.com/books-and-publications/book/winner-take-all

Lions on the move, McKinsey Global,
file:///Users/wmworia/Documents/Afrinnovator/Essays/MGI_Lions_on_the_move_african_economies_full_report.pdf

Tullow Says Kenya Oil Find May Be East Africa's Largest,
Wall Street Journal, http://online.wsj.com/article/BT-CO-20120507-709361.html

SA Ten Year Innovation Plan,
http://www.innovationeasterncape.co.za/download/sa_ten_year_innovation_plan.pdf

INSEAD Global Innovation Index,
http://www.wipo.int/freepublications/en/economics/gii_2012.pdf

The iHub UX Lab and Supercomputer Cluster, Erik
Hersman, http://whiteafrican.com/2012/05/23/the-ihub-ux-lab-and-supercomputer-cluster/

The Role of Governments in Promoting Technology and Innovation in Africa

By Will Mutua

We live in a time when many governments are facing tremendous pressures, externally and internally. In many countries, citizens have risen up against mediocre and unfair leadership. The Arab Spring is one of the most evident examples of this. The question of leadership and in many cases, the lack thereof, has gone unanswered. Technology has played a key role in empowering citizens like never before; they are finding online avenues to express their dissatisfaction with oppressive and unfair regimes on blogs and social media.

It goes without saying that governments and leadership set the stage and the pace at which a country progresses or retrogresses. The question of government and governance and what is appropriate government/governance is critical - just as an unfair and oppressive regime can cause countless negative effects for citizens, so can a fair and just one create positive effects.

We live in a world with leadership vacuums in many areas. It has been said that everything rises and falls on leadership. The crucial role of leadership in any context, and specifically in innovation has led to countless conferences. Earlier this year, for example, Nokia held the second edition of its Open Innovation Africa Summit with the central theme being that of leadership in innovation.

In the past, one of Africa's most daunting challenges was that of leadership, or more precisely, political leadership. There's a time when coups and civil wars were the order of the day across multiple African states. The situation today is not 100% ok, but there's a radical difference between the Africa of the 90s and the Africa of today. The 2010 McKinsey "*Lions on the Move: The progress and potential of African economies*" report underscores the important role played by government in the process of overturning Africa's fortunes:

"… *More important were government actions to end political conflicts, improve macroeconomic conditions, and create better business climates, which enabled growth to accelerate broadly across countries and sectors.*" (Page 1 of the report)

Perhaps the most important action taken by governments in African states is to end armed conflicts. According to the same McKinsey report, the average number of serious conflicts in Africa (i.e. those resulting in over 1000 deaths per year) has reduced by almost 50% between the 90s and the 2000s. Countries such as Angola have in recent times posted record growth levels as a result of ending years of armed conflicts, creating the necessary stability for business to take place. Indeed, Angola is one of the darlings of the Chinese as far as their investing in Africa goes. Some of these countries are growing from very low bases given the destruction of infrastructure, loss and displacement of people that took place through years of armed conflict, but the establishment of peace and order is creating a favorable environment for them to accelerate growth rapidly.

Governments' efforts have led to an average reduction of inflation rates from around 22% per annum in the 90s to 8% in the 2000s, reduction of government debt to GDP ratio from close to 82% in the 90s to 59% in the 2000s and shrinking budget deficits from 4.6% of GDP to 1.8%. The actions of such individuals as Fred Swaniker, through his African Leadership University present the promise of producing even better leadership for the African continent in future.

Turning to the specific subject matter of this book, what is the role of government as far as technology and innovation are concerned? In general, the role of governments can be summarized in three broad areas: the government as a Promoter, a Producer and a Consumer of technology. Let's take a look at these areas in some detail:

The Government as a Promoter of Technology and Innovation

We've already taken a look at how critical it is for government to create a stable environment as far as politics is concerned. This is the baseline upon which the government can build to promote technology and innovation in a country. Without a peaceful environment in which the rule of law is upheld, not much productivity can take place.

NOTE: The aim here is not to prescribe specific actions or policies that a government can apply but consider from a broad perspective the areas through which a government can look into in order to create appropriate, country-specific, context-specific policies and actions that promote technology innovation in that country.

There are four other broad areas through which government can create a suitable environment thereby promoting tech and innovation:

1. Legal Environment

A sound, legal environment ensures predictability for investors, particularly foreign investors, and safeguards their interests. If the legal framework is sound for carrying out business and the government demonstrates that the rule of law is upheld and applied fairly across the board, investors can gain a sense of security, predictability and comfort in knowing that things cannot change at the drop of a hat, or that some player will have an unfair advantage by having special ties to government.

A key part of the legal framework that applies to innovation is Intellectual Property Rights (IPR) and sufficient enforcement of the same. Why go ahead and make significant investments in time, money and effort to R&D and create some innovation if someone else could just sit by, watch and eventually copy your innovation? Innovators need to know that they have the security to benefit from their innovations.

The issue of creating a suitable legal environment can at times be tricky. A government needs to strike that elusive "goldilocks zone" where it creates a balanced legal framework - one that is not loose, weak and unpredictable; and at the same time not too stringent that it stifles economic and innovative activity.

2. Fiscal Environment

Through its fiscal policy and wise application of revenues obtained from taxation, a government can further promote innovative activity within the country. Some key areas a government can focus on to create a huge impact are:

a. Education and Human Capital Development: A highly educated and skilled workforce is imperative to transitioning into a knowledge-based economy. Without adequate skilled human capital it is impossible to move an economy forward in high tech industries that are knowledge intensive. For example, it is estimated that the number of researchers in Africa accounts for only 2.2% of the total number of researchers globally, as per the UNESCO 2010 Science Report. According to the June

2011 edition of Nature, Uganda has only 25 researchers per million inhabitants; as per the UNESCO report, as at 2007 South Africa boasted about 392 researchers per million inhabitants while the rest of sub-Saharan Africa averaged 57.5 researchers per million. Contrast these figures with India – 136.9, China – 1070.9, Europe – 2638.7, North America – 4624.4 and Japan –5573 researchers per million inhabitants.

In addition, universities can become hotbeds of innovation and research. One can consider, for example, Stanford University's effect in Silicon Valley.

b. Providing grants for research activity: In 2007, the African Union set a standard for governments to spend at least 1% of GDP on R&D. In the same year, only South Africa, Uganda and Malawi managed to meet the standard. In absolute terms the South African government spends the most on R&D out of all the countries in Africa. Overall, Africa spends a fraction of a percentage on R&D. Governments can promote innovation by supporting R&D through grants, building of infrastructure (research universities, research labs) and other such activities.

c. Foreign Direct Investment: Creating an accommodating environment that allows free flow of FDI into the country can open up the country to foreign investment in technology industries. Across Africa, the trend is positive though - the number of FDI projects in Africa grew 27% from 2010 to 2011, and has grown at a compound rate of close to 20% since 2007; intra-African FDI has expanded at a compounded rate of 42% since 2007. However, much more could be done; Africa's share of global FDI projects amounts to only 5.5% of the total.

d. Grants for Capital Investment: The government can extend grants to subsidize capital-intensive activities such as building plants, acquiring equipment and other physical investments. Countries such as Ireland have successfully used grants to attract high tech firms Intel and Dell to set up in the country.

e. Venture Capital and Private Equity Support: Ease of access to capital is critical to entrepreneurial activity. VC is particularly key in high-risk investments. Governments can extend special incentives for VC/PE activity; for example, in China venture capitalists investing in high tech business may offset 70% of their investment against future income. Such benefits promote private investment in tech.

3. Tax Incentives

Governments can promote innovation by selectively applying different kinds of tax incentives to achieve different outcomes as far as promoting technology and innovation is concerned. In emerging and advanced knowledge-based economies, a wide array of tax incentives can usually be found, usually applied very selectively to promote specific goals.

Specific tax incentives that reward corporations for, say, carrying out R&D, or that make it easier to bring in foreign skilled labor, or those that promote Venture Capital activity, or other specific action by the investor/innovator/entrepreneur help balance out the risk/reward equation. Appropriate tax incentives can make the difference between an investor taking some calculated risk or not by reducing the risk side of the equation and relatively increasing the reward side. Tax incentives can also be used to promote specific kinds of innovative activity based on a country's comparative advantage to others or even direct innovative activities to certain geographical regions.

4. Infrastructure Development

The government (in collaboration with private enterprise) can do a lot to improve the infrastructural condition of a country and, in so doing, promote innovation. This is very important particularly in Africa. In general, insufficient infrastructural capacity has been cited as a key challenge to Africa's economic progress. It's estimated that $360 billion worth of investment will be needed over the next 25 years or so to take care of Africa's infrastructure needs. In fact, infrastructure development is one of the biggest opportunities for investment in Africa.

An obvious example of how governments can make the right commitments to infrastructural development that can in turn open up a country and turn up the innovative capacities of its people is the undersea fiber projects that, in just a few years, have turned the continent from virtually being unconnected to the rest of the world via undersea fiber to being almost too connected. In times past, the cost of Internet access in many African countries was exorbitant and inhibitive to carrying out business effectively, particularly for heavily Internet-reliant sectors such as Business Process Outsourcing.

Another illustration is the fact that in some countries, electricity is either extremely unreliable or extremely expensive. According to a PriceWaterhouseCooper survey of CEOs in Nigeria, energy cost was one of their main causes of concern e.g. Telcos are estimated to spend 45.9 billion Naira (or about USD 311 million) on fuel generators. At the same time, the government is enacting higher electricity tariffs.

The Government as a Producer of Technology and Innovation

Government can itself become a key producer of technology and innovation. Through public research institutions, for example, they can churn out significant innovations.

However, the aim of governments in innovation is usually different from that of the private sector. The private sector usually looks out not just for innovation, but also commercial viability of innovations; there is a strong market focus. The aim is usually to create something the investor/entrepreneur/innovator can profit from and so there is a key focus on whether there is market demand for the product, if there isn't then it's not worth pursuing - at least as far as for-profit initiatives go.

Government on the other hand usually seeks to serve broader socio-political and national causes where the primary focus is not to introduce the outcome of innovative activity to the market. Take the US goal of landing a man on the moon as an example - the key goal and measure of success as far as the government was concerned was the nationalistic goal of getting a man on the moon and back - not whether the technology could be brought to market for the purpose of say, space tourism (or indeed the commercial application of countless other technologies and innovations that were no doubt created in the process of landing a man on the moon and bringing him back safely). The task of finding commercial application of space technology is largely being handled by private enterprise such as Sir Richard Branson's Virgin Galactic.

All the same, governmental Research and Development through public research institutes, for example, can produce innovation. Private enterprise can then come in and figure out how to apply the outcome of governmental innovation to the market. At the same time, creating such public research institutes could increase the capacity of the country for research by, for example, creating the specialized facilities required for high level research and creating a demand for specialized skills, so someone who, say, wants to study space technologies knows they can be absorbed into such facilities and find employment within their own country.

The Government as a Consumer of Technology and Innovation

Government can also promote technology and innovation by consuming indigenous innovation. Indeed, government can be a significant consumer of innovative, locally produced products and services through public procurement. For example, in Kenya, an innovative team of young ladies founded a startup called M-Farm that applies mobile telephony innovatively in supporting farmers and agribusiness. Where the government's aims of promoting agribusiness (which is a major contributor to the economy of a country such as Kenya) coincide with the use of mobile technology, the government could procure M-Farm's services instead of developing their own solution to the same problem.

As we have seen, government can do a lot to support local innovation, in Africa and beyond. There are multiple ways through which the government can create a suitable environment for innovation and even become an active participant in the creation of innovative services. Hopefully we will see more governments doing so in Africa.

References:

Best and Worst Countries to do Business in Africa, Global Post,
http://www.globalpost.com/dispatch/news/regions/africa/12
0523/best-and-worst-countries-do-business-africa-
interactive

Lions on the move: The progress and potential of African economies, McKinsey Global Institute,
http://www.mckinsey.com/insights/mgi/research/productivi
ty_competitiveness_and_growth/lions_on_the_move

Building Bridges Ernst & Young's 2012 Africa Attractiveness Survey,
http://www.ey.com/ZA/en/Issues/Business-
environment/2012-Africa-attractiveness-survey

Government's many roles in fostering innovation, PriceWaterhouseCooper,
http://www.pwc.com/gx/en/technology/publications/govern
ments-role-in-fostering-innovation.jhtml

Building Innovation Systems, Phillip A. Griffits,
http://sig.ias.edu/files/pdfs/IAC_Innovation_2_05.pdf

Infrastructure, resources and consumer demand – Africa's three main opportunities, Dapo Okubadejo, http://www.howwemadeitinafrica.com/infrastructure-resources-and-consumer-demand-%E2%80%93-africas-three-main-opportunities/18098/

Africa needs $360bn basic infrastructure investment over 25 years, http://nepadwatercoe.org/africa-needs-360bn-basic-infrastructure-investment-over-25-years/

Upturn for African technology investment, Nature Journal, http://www.nature.com/news/2011/110526/full/news.2011.320.html

Telcos to fuel generators with N46bn this year, http://www.businessdayonline.com/NG/index.php/news/76-hot-topic/35304-telcos-to-fuel-generators-with-n46bn-this-year

Nigeria: Despite Challenges, CEOs Foresee Brighter Future, http://allafrica.com/stories/201204090260.html

Nigeria, Are You Ready For Increased Electricity Tariff? New Tariff to Take Effect in June 2012, Adeola Adeyemo, http://www.bellanaija.com/2012/05/11/nigeria-are-you-ready-for-increased-electricity-tariff-new-tariff-to-take-effect-in-june-2012/

Africa's Technology Parks & Cities Arms Race - Is it worth it?

By Mbwana Alliy

One of the most debated topics in IT innovation industrial policy is the place of tech parks and cities catalyzed by African Government's role in helping lay down important infrastructure.

Kenya's Konza Tech city is slated to cost $7B. Tanzania's Rhapta's city is meant to cost maybe $1B or so. I even got wind of an Angola mega city project slated to cost $10B that includes a tech park. Rwanda and Uganda are also planning tech parks or cities of their own if they have not begun pushing so.

Each tech city or park has different ambition levels. The main objective in these projects tends to originate from the idea that foreign companies will set up their regional headquarters and create jobs, as well as the idea that lots of local medium-sized ICT firms and business process outsourcing centers will emerge and move in. The model is to emulate the parks that have gone up in Bangalore, India.

Tech parks and cities also can be financed and paid back from the real estate development model. They are "safe investments" for the expensive grand projects they are.

However, the premise held by government officials that these cities would create armies of entrepreneurs and innovation based on this infrastructure may be flawed thinking. Did Mark Zuckerberg or Larry Page need a gleaming tech city to create Google or Facebook? Or was it a coincidence that these founders originated from world-class universities-Stanford and Harvard? Similarly, what is the role of the Indian Institutes of Technology (IIT) in India in their tech industry?

To be clear, Tech parks and cities do have their benefits. For one, the economic zones and incentives created should draw some companies to set up there vs. the growing, overcrowded and traffic-jammed cities. The infrastructure itself can help isolate many problems that plague firms in normal city areas. This includes reliable Internet and electrical power as well as good transportation links. Local data center investments to enable cloud computing will clearly benefit everyone and start to take advantage of all that unused bandwidth capacity emerging in Africa. Infrastructure is important. China's investments across

Africa for instance are essential to both itself and to aid countries that are aiming for growth- not to mention these projects create jobs just to set up in the short term. It's very similar to winning the bid for the Olympics or the World Cup - when executed correctly, the expansion to the economy can be substantial and long lasting in the region.

Tech park initiatives tend to be led by governments whose political objectives can at times trump any real sense of how to really enable innovation and entrepreneurship, which involves a lot of cultural incentives and a particular focus on improving education. They often ignore economics and the laws of supply and demand. For instance, how many regional offices can Microsoft and Google set up in East Africa when each city is trying to build its own billion-dollar tech park? An outsourcing center still builds a dependency on western market economies, and what happens when another region gains cost advantages just as people are now moving away from India? Or the big companies want to move these functions back onto their own shores or even just invest in their own corporate offices?

Take Dubai as an example, they created a gleaming city out of the desert with its vast oil wealth and created an Internet

City which did attract companies such as Microsoft, Oracle and Cisco. These tech companies mainly created sales and customer services offices for the EMEA region. There was very little R&D and hence innovation. But how many entrepreneurs and groundbreaking innovations resulted? How can you expect innovation from Dubai when failure and risk-taking in business is treated so negatively? Meanwhile, their neighbor, Israel, even with its conflict problems, is able to attract direct investment from tech companies like Intel and the country, by far, punches above its weight in innovation in the tech sector. It is really, a Startup Nation. More Israeli tech companies are listed on the NASDAQ exchange than all of the companies in Europe combined, and the country has access to more Venture Capital per capita than any other nation on earth. What makes them different? The answer is simple: trained and risk taking human resources.

Here's a thought: *If you are planning to build world class football team, do you first build a 100,000 seat stadium or work to recruit coaches, find and nurture talent or even continue to stimulate the pride of football in the country?*

An alternative approach to this top-down kind of strategy is a bottom-up grassroots approach that appeals to the entrepreneur and hacker grounds where universities *are* the infrastructure, vs. the corporate mindset of "gleaming campuses" being the infrastructure. This kind of approach, however, is harder to achieve but has more long lasting results in creating homegrown tech firms and spurring real, indigenous innovation.

Another aspect regarding tech parks and cities is the tendency to try to "create a whole ecosystem" from scratch, including world-class universities and residential areas for the human resources. An all-inclusive city makes a lot of sense, especially the university inclusion for reasons I just mentioned, but then the bigger the scope the more likely governments underestimate how much effort and time this really requires, not to mention execution.

Creating a fancy building or city does not foster entrepreneurship. History has shown this. Assuming the parks are built, we may find that many become ghost towns in the short term if no talent develops to fill them.

To be fair, tech parks are not worthless endeavors in Africa. They do have a place and fill critical infrastructure needs, but to depend on them for more than they can actually deliver, such as a source of innovation and entrepreneurship is deeply flawed. More of this money and effort would go further to encourage entrepreneurship, attract venture capital firms by creating sound policies and, last but certainly not least, invest in an educated workforce. The dividends will pay off in time, not overnight.

Singapore, through its *Spring Singapore Initiative* and Chile, through the *Startup Chile Initiative* stand out as countries that seem to be making excellent strides and are thinking outside the box; they use human resource incentives over gleaming cities to lure talent, which in turn, helps infuse a Silicon Valley like culture.

References:

Konza City, http://www.konzacity.co.ke/

Tanzania Answers to Konza Technology City With "Raphta City", http://utnc.org/wordpress/2011/04/tanzania-answers-to-konza-technology-city-with-%E2%80%9Craphta-city%E2%80%9D/

Bangalore International Tech Park, http://www.itpbangalore.com/

Plug and Play Tech Center,
http://www.plugandplaytechcenter.com/

Indian Institute of Technology, http://www.iitd.ac.in/

Kenya: When in Nairobi, You Rush to Beat the Traffic,
Sam Ruburika,
http://allafrica.com/stories/200906160747.html

Investment in Infrastructure Crucial to Africa's Economic
Growth,
http://www.voanews.com/english/news/africa/Investment-
In-Infrastructure-Crucial-to-Africas-Economic-
Growth030211-117248018.html

Dubai Internet City, http://www.dubaiinternetcity.com/

Startup Nation: The Story of Israelis Economic Miracle,
http://www.startupnationbook.com/

SPRING Singapore,
http://www.spring.gov.sg/Pages/Homepage.aspx

StartUp Chile, http://www.startupchile.org/

Does the "Copy to/Clone..." Strategy Work in Africa?

By Mbwana Alliy

One can be tempted to think regarding technology startups in Africa: *why not just use the "copy to" strategy?* Clone an eBay, clone a Groupon... After all there are thousands of Groupon clones in China! The Samwer brothers in Germany, for instance, are notorious for doing this so well, it angers many innovators in America.

This strategy, however, is not as easy to implement as it sounds, even though it does work in some cases. Here are a few pointers on why and when this strategy can or can't work. It often comes down to the need for *local* or *incremental* innovation:

Technology Adoption Cycle is not necessarily the same everywhere - Focus on the fundamental need

Job sites like Jobberman in Nigeria are in many ways direct clones of other job sites around the world. Why does cloning a jobs site work so well, almost anywhere you try one? Job search is a fundamental need all over the world and the profiles of job seekers looking for high value jobs ,as well as recruiters are somewhat global and standardized in nature e.g. entry positions out of university, the use of English as the language of business etc. But the key thing is that both sides of a 2-sided marketplace are pretty technology savvy and can use a computer to both post and search for a job. Paul Bassat, whose company, SEEK, is a top brand in the jobs site market in Australia, for example, understands what it takes to make job sites work, no matter the context, so he is perfectly positioned to act both as a cloner and investor and has indeed been successful in other parts of the world, including China and Brazil.

When does this not work? When there is a fundamental mismatch in tech adoption and assumptions on business models. It's easy for a foreigner to assume western notions as a given for African consumers and businesses, but even resident techies in Africa often forget their target customers are not like them. Take the case of social media marketing in the African context: some companies have never used traditional marketing before, or they believe that a billboard ad is by far the most effective way to advertise because "big gorilla company next door" does it, so it must work! Attention can sometimes be the number one issue for companies trying to deliver marketing solutions to businesses, try live in the African business's shoes for a while before you try push your whizz bang social media, SMS marketing solution; you'll find that small businesses in particular are very busy running their business to spend up to a day learning your technology for a benefit they can't quantify yet.

In Africa, although people are used to paying for utilities - airtime and some services - through mobile payments, the leap to do so for things like travel tickets etc comes down to trust/fraud fear factors in commerce which are still lagging behind the technology's actual effectiveness. It's only a matter of time till this situation changes as everyone gets used to transacting online. As for business models, as an example, transaction fee models may not always be the best way to go in Africa because the initial volumes needed can be very high.

Another way to look at this is through an economic lens: customer acquisition cost and time. This can be very high or lengthy since you are actually investing a ton in customer education of, say, "why SMS marketing is effective", then once customers adopt your solution and finally get it 6 months later, they may stick around forever and their referral to their friends' or relatives' business becomes easier. So in many cases, it's a "last man standing" play, at some point the adoption picks up and whoever is left around wins and wins big, dominating the market. Add a payment wall and you often increase your adoption barrier. This is why "freemium", models are so popular. You don't need to get paid at the same time that your customer has to "learn" that your solution is worth it.

Design Thinking and Focus on Product

This is a major factor: simply a back to basics focus on design. Just because *Groupon* works around the world doesn't mean it will work the same way everywhere for mobile-first Sub-Saharan Africa. Even on the normal web, when you analyze commerce sites in India and China, they look very different in style from their western counterparts. Smart startups trying to clone or copy understand this. Take the obvious - feature phone ubiquity - and importance in designing for bandwidth-constrained environments. We see this first hand with the growth of mobile social networks such as *Mxit*. A strong focus on design for unique environments can help foster better products that can get adopted faster.

Local Execution is Key

Back to commerce: when you take a look at India, you quickly realize that the Cash on Delivery (CoD) model is an essential ingredient for e-commerce in that market, even though many Indians own credit cards, there is still a huge trust factor. Whilst we have mobile payments in Africa, m-commerce on a comparable to Amazon or eBay won't be fulfilled until we sort out the fulfillment part of the equation. India solved the payment, fulfillment and fraud issues in one go as in the case of *FlipKart*. So a clone of, say, eBay or Amazon even with mobile money simply won't work in Sub-Saharan Africa until the complete fulfillment puzzle is solved in the way India solved it. One could ask whether CoD clones to Sub-Saharan Africa may be the solution to kick starting a bigger m-commerce revolution. There's a good example in Tanzania - a form of CoD (more like delivery on payment) + mobile payments that actually mirrors a traditional western style e-commerce transaction- you can order Dodoma Wine from the vineyards by calling and paying via M-PESA and it would be shipped by bus and you'd get alerted to pick it up from the Bus Station. This already works and is in use, with more careful design, could it be scaled up for the masses and for other goods? It's easy to fall into the trap of assuming it might without questioning all the assumptions and going through a more investigative design process.

Of course these factors are in fact intertwined. A compelling product designed for the right audience in Africa and executed in a local manner is what works and simultaneously lowers acquisition cost and time; otherwise one is bound to face a long process of educating the customer on "how the west does it and so you should do it too." As we well know, Africa is not Europe or America.

So does the "Copy to" Strategy work? Yes – if executed carefully with some of the factors we've looked at being taken into careful consideration.

Some startups don't have the funding, expertise or patience to sustain this and often get impatient and distracted. Some of the smart and persistent ones actually figure out the bottleneck that is slowing down their business and directly solve it for themselves, sometimes discovering a whole new business there as they realize it's a problem someone else has. In the end it actually comes down to innovation. Even if incremental, innovating appropriately can make an idea in one context work in the other.

References:

Samwer Brothers, http://www.quora.com/What-do-people-know-about-the-Samwer-Brothers-of-the-European-Founders-Fund

Jobberman Nigeria, http://www.jobberman.com/

Fraud slows down uptake of mobile money payments, David Mugwe, http://www.businessdailyafrica.com/Fraud+slows+down+uptake+of+mobile+money+payments++/-/539552/1392366/-/bqlk6gz/-/index.html

Stanford Program on Liberation Technology, http://liberationtechnology.stanford.edu/

Joshua Cohen, http://liberationtechnology.stanford.edu/people/Joshua_Cohen/

FlipKart, http://www.flipkart.com/

Research and Development in Sub-Saharan Africa: The Current Situation

By Will Mutua

In 2007, an African Union Summit set a goal of spending at least 1% of GDP on Research and Development by 2010. According to the *Africa Innovation Outlook 2010* report from NEPAD, only 3 countries managed the feat - South Africa, Uganda and Malawi. In absolute terms, South Africa spent the highest amount on R&D, 30 times more than Malawi and 8 times more than Nigeria, to form the big three spenders in R&D in Africa. Against the backdrop of other regions in the world, Africa has a low investment rate in R&D in terms of spending as a percentage of R&D. Here are the 2010 numbers as per PricewaterhouseCoopers' *"Government's Many Roles in Fostering Innovation"* report:

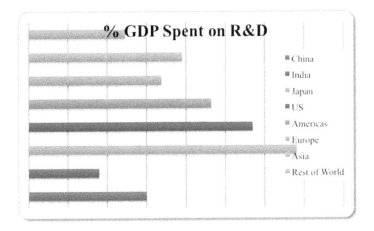

Figure 12: R&D Spending

The Challenges

Several challenges have hampered the rapid growth of R&D in Africa, key among these being:

Funding Constraints

One of the key concerns as far as promoting R&D is concerned is that of funding. As we have already seen, most countries spend a very small fraction of their GDP in R&D. In addition, many countries are dependent on, usually intermittent, foreign funding. For example, about 38% of R&D funding in Tanzania and Senegal comes from abroad. According to the *UNESCO Science Report 2010,* the proportion of GDP devoted to R&D averages about 0.3% on the continent.

Brain Drain & Lack of Human Capacity

Brain drain is a classical problem in Africa. Few students who acquire specialized skills having studied in foreign countries return to their home countries to apply their skills. Many times it is because of a lack of opportunities to apply their skills back home, or many times they become overqualified and cannot be absorbed into companies in their home countries. In Uganda, for example, there are only an estimated 25 researchers per million inhabitants, in Senegal, more than 50% of its agricultural researchers were over 50 years old in 2007, partly as a result of a slump in spending for higher education and research in the late 1980s and early 1990s. According to the previously cited UNESCO report, in 2009, at least a third of African scientists or those with engineering degrees were living and working in developed countries!

We have previously taken a look at the critical role played by the right kind of education in spurring innovation in a nation (See chapter "*Africa and Innovation: Nature and Nurture - Education*") The fact of the matter is, without a critical number of individuals undertaking the right kind of education that equips them with the necessary skills and allows them to pursue their curiosities and creative abilities to their maximum capacity in the right kind of environment, Africa will still lag behind in R&D. Significant steps have been taken to improve enrollment at the primary school level, following the *Millennium Development Goals*, and some steps forward have also been made at the secondary level but tertiary education requires a lot of attention.

Infrastructural Capacity

Another big challenge is the lack of infrastructural capacity in terms of there being enough and well-equipped research facilities. In Uganda, for example, only 6 out of 27 universities offer science-related programs; and even at those few universities, only one in five students pursues a degree in science. There is a lack of adequately equipped laboratories and labs in universities, making it difficult for students to carry on practical and productive learning. This is especially the case in countries that have only very recently emerged from years of civil war and internal political strife. In other cases, appropriate Internet access is missing, as well as inadequate ICT infrastructure. In a globalized world, collaboration and cooperation in R&D is more important than ever; not having the tools to do this severely impedes the capacity of universities to engage and contribute to the global body of knowledge.

Possible Solutions

A lot can be done to spur more R&D across Sub-Saharan Africa, both from the public and private sectors. Going into detail on specific measures is outside the scope of this particular publication; the aim here is simply to highlight some of the major problems and some of the measures that can be taken to remedy the situation. Among the measures that can be taken include:

1. More commitment from governments to prioritize and consequently allocate larger proportions of national budgets to R&D could directly help to solve the funding issue.

2. Governments can also do quite a bit to incentivize private sector R&D by, for example, creating tax incentives and subsidies for companies engaging in R&D, or by creating favorable conditions for Foreign Direct Investment in R&D intensive areas. In addition, creating favorable policy environment and other kind of incentives that make it easier for foreign high-tech companies to set up in the country

and engage in R&D will help. (*See the chapter on government role in promoting innovation*)

3. Increasing the amount of collaboration between local research institutes and foreign ones could significantly increase output in terms of the number of scientific publications, for instance.

4. Finally, engaging the African diaspora and tapping into their specialized skills, knowledge and knowledge networks or even drawing them back into the continent entirely could greatly shift things in a very positive direction.

A good indication that things are headed in the right direction is the recently held *Africa Forum on Science, Technology and Innovation* (STI), the first of its kind in Africa. The forum brought together stakeholders with the aim of taking a look at the current state of STI on the continent and how to further promote the same. One of its outcomes was a written declaration by government ministers of science and related ministries from several African states that amongst other things promises to:

- Pursue the creation, strengthening and implementation of policies that will foster STI development.

- Enhance the linkage between Science Technology Engineering & Mathematics (STEM) Education and Labor Markets in Africa.

- Strengthen linkages between knowledge generation and enterprise development.

- Strengthen Scientific Research in Africa by promoting and increasing investment in collaborative research.

- Come up with ways to harness STI for sustainable development.

References:

The African Manifesto for Science, Technology and Innovation, African Technology Policy Studies Network,

http://www.atpsnet.org/Files/the_african_manifesto_for_st
&i.pdf

Science in Africa: The view from the front line, Nature
Journal,
http://www.nature.com/news/2011/110629/full/474556a.ht
ml

Upturn for African technology investment, Nature Journal,
http://www.nature.com/news/2011/110526/full/news.2011.
320.html

African Innovation Outlook 2010, NEPAD,
http://www.nepad.org/humancapitaldevelopment/knowledg
e/doc/2226/african-innovation-outlook-2010-executive-
summary

Global Research Report - Africa, Thomson Reuters,
http://thomsonreuters.com/content/corporate/docs/globalres
earchreport-africa.pdf

Governments Many Roles in Fostering Innovation,
PriceWaterhouseCooper,
http://www.ey.com/Publication/vwLUAssets/EY_2012_Afr
ica_attractiveness_survey/$FILE/attractiveness_2012_afric
a_v17.pdf

Research and Development: Africa is making progress despite major challenges, UNESCO, http://www.unesco.org/new/en/media-services/single-view/news/research_and_development_africa_is_making_progress_despite_major_challenges/

Science Report 2010, UNESCO, http://www.unesco.org/new/en/natural-sciences/science-technology/prospective-studies/unesco-science-report/unesco-science-report-2010/

Closing the R&D gap in African health care, McKinsey Quarterly, https://www.mckinseyquarterly.com/Closing_the_RD_gap_in_African_health_care_2593

South Africa's Research and Development Profile, SAccess, http://www.saccess-project.eu/downloads/South_Africa_R&D_Profile_(10-02-2011).pdf

African Universities and the Challenge of Research Capacity Development, Akilagpa Sawyerr, http://www.codesria.org/IMG/pdf/8-SAWYERR.pdf

Brain Drain in Africa, Wikipedia, http://en.wikipedia.org/wiki/Brain_drain#Africa

Doctor brain drain costs Africa $2 billion, Reuters, http://www.reuters.com/article/2011/11/25/us-african-doctors-migration-idUSTRE7AO00O20111125

Brain Drain in Africa, Joint Statement by the Network of African Science Academies (NASAC), 2009, http://www.nationalacademies.org/includes/NASACbraindrain09.pdf

Reversing Africa's 'brain drain', Gumisai Mutume, Africa Recovery Magazine, http://www.un.org/en/africarenewal/vol17no2/172brain.htm

The Challenges of Financing Research in Institutions of Higher Education in Africa, Prof. Ngothowa Kariuki, http://gc.aau.org/papers/ngotho_wa_kariuki_full20.pdf

Africa's journey to space begins on the ground, Meredith Baker, BBC News, http://www.bbc.co.uk/news/business-18739694

First Africa Forum on Science Technology and Innovations in Nairobi, UNESCO, http://www.unesco.org/new/en/media-services/single-view/news/first_africa_forum_on_science_technology_and_innovations_in_nairobi/

Nairobi Ministerial Declaration on Science Technology and Innovation,

http://www.adeanet.org/STIforum/en/content/nairobi-ministerial-declaration

Part 2: In Search of a Model for Technology Innovation and Entrepreneurship Ecosystems that fits the African Context

The Making of Silicon Valleys in Africa

By Will Mutua

Many studies have been done on what it takes to create an innovation ecosystem in a particular geographic area. The concept of National Innovation Systems has been with us for some time now. Many nations seek to emulate the success of vibrant innovation ecosystems, chief amongst them being Silicon Valley. In Africa, terms such as 'Silicon Savannah' (referring to the eastern part of Africa) or 'Silicon Cape' (referring to South Africa and Cape Town in particular) have been coined to capture the efforts being made to turn these regions into the same kind of startup and innovation culture and ecosystem embodied in Silicon Valley.

However, it goes without saying that creating such an ecosystem is easier said than done. Silicon Valley itself has been in the making for decades (since the 1940s and the 2nd World War actually - see references "The Secret History of Silicon Valley") and has evolved through many cycles to become what we see today, and indeed, it is still evolving.

In Africa, two broad approaches are being taken to try to achieve this result, coming from virtually opposite directions. Time will tell what will work best and be the most efficient in the long run.

What are these two approaches?

I. The Top Down Approach

This is the approach being taken particularly by governments across the continent. Nation after nation have in recent times announced ambitious plans to build tech parks and tech cities, with the aim of drawing in multinational technology companies to set up engineering and research facilities and in the process spur local innovation in these special areas that are set apart specifically for this cause.

These projects are huge endeavors drawing in multiple stakeholders and involving massive budgets. Here are just a few of those projects:

a. Konza City in Kenya (konza.co.ke): Konza City is to be built about 64km from the capital city of Kenya, Nairobi across an expanse of 2000 hectares. It will feature a technology park, science park, universities, a business district as well as residential and other commercial areas.

The project is estimated to cost USD 14.5 billion, and will take 20 years to complete (though the actual development will take a phased approach)

b. Rhapta City in Tanzania, Dar es Salaam: A public-private partnership (PPP) initiative by the Tanzania Commission for Science and Technology (COSTECH)

c. Africa Premier Innovation Corridor (APIC) in Abuja, Nigeria: A science and technology park proposed by the Nigerian National Office for Technology Acquisition and Promotion (NOTAP) and the Abuja Geographic Information Systems (AGIS).

This approach is largely a top-down approach, with governments setting the pace and determining what will go where and when. They are also premised on the idea that if you build the infrastructure, the rest will follow, somewhat akin to first building the railway tracks and assuming the rest will follow.

There are pros and cons to this approach however. (Mbwana Alliy has done a great job at analyzing this approach in a the chapter, *"The Africa Tech Parks & Cities Arms Race - Is it worth it?"*)

Pros

1. If (and in some cases this can be a big IF) governments can get the right leadership in place to spearhead these projects, they can have good outcomes. The problem in some instances is that if you combine poor leadership with a multi-million or billion dollar budget, the chances of corruption, and consequently either having the budget doubling in the process, or the process being stretched over a longer time than anticipated go up. In addition, the leaders need to have a realistic understanding of what can and can't be achieved through these projects.

2. Since these projects are spearheaded by governments, the government can, through it's sheer clout, bring together the right investors to fund the projects, as well as create the right partnerships, as well as establish the goodwill for multinationals to buy into the project.

3. These parks can provide a central location where the government can apply specific measures such as tax breaks and other incentives that promote innovative activity. They can also result in fairly efficient 'zones' focused on some particular activities e.g. traffic can be better controlled within the area, critical amenities such as reliable electricity can be guaranteed within a central area that's relatively small versus the rest of the country etc

Cons

1. As previously stated, leadership is a two sided coin, if it so happens that the wrong kind of leadership is involved in spearheading these projects, the results can be disastrous.

2. At times, these projects are painted as silver bullets that can achieve more than they feasibly can. As Mbwana notes, for example, it may not be that simply putting up buildings and other infrastructure will necessarily, magically, transform the local culture to a startup/innovation/entrepreneurial culture if it wasn't already so. In which case the key outcome of such cities will be the creation of sites for business process outsourcing companies or sales offices for foreign companies.

3. The economics of these projects can sometimes be questionable. For example, why build a tech park in Kenya and another in Tanzania with the aim of drawing the same set of multinationals to come in and set up in either country? In addition, questions have been raised, in some instances, about governments seeking out foreign investors to put up the financing for parts of these projects while overlooking potential local investors that could do the same job.

II. The Bottom Up Approach

This approach is well embodied in the rise of tech and innovation hubs across Africa. In the last few years, multiple tech and innovation hubs have sprang up all over the continent.

In Nairobi, for example, there are as many as 5 or more hubs within about 5 km of the Nairobi Innovation Hub (iHub), the pioneer tech hub in Africa.

Hub	City, Country	Founded	Website
ActivSpaces	Buea, Cameroon	February, 2010	http://activspaces.com
Banta Labs	St. Louis, Senegal	April, 2011	http://bantalabs.com
Hive Colab	Kampala, Uganda	March, 2011	http://hivecolab.com
iHub	Nairobi, Kenya	March, 2010	http://ihub.co.ke
NaiLab	Nairobi, Kenya	January, 2011	http://ilab.co.ke

Botswan a Innovatio n Hub	Gaborone, Botswana	2006	http://bih.co.b w
Ice Ethiopia (IceAddi s)	Addis Ababa, Ethiopia	January, 2011	http://ice-ethiopia.org
BongoHi ve	Lusaka, Zambia	2011	
Umbono	Cape Town, South Africa	March, 2011	http://www.go ogle.co.za/intl/ en/umbono/
iLab Liberia	Liberia	2011	http://ilabliber ia.com

Table 4: Some tech hubs in Africa

The premise with tech hubs is what you could call, "feeding the bottom of the pyramid". The idea is that innovation starts at the grassroots, so to speak; it starts with those two co-founders who have an idea and just need the basics - the right skills, some mentorship, a place to sit, the right environment and an internet connection - to get started. That's how Google got started, and Yahoo or Facebook or anyone of many of the iconic tech giants of today. The hubs also aim at creating the right environment - one that celebrates and encourages innovation, one that tolerates failure and starting up again, one that draws in other players e.g. investors and one that creates the space and opportunity for 'co-mingling' of different people, from different backgrounds and different skills with the idea that great things happen when great people get together.

Unlike tech parks and cities which are government-backed and involve massive budgets, hubs are usually private sector-backed and involve much lower investment levels.

Building a Silicon Valley

So which approach will work best? Which will produce the next Silicon Valley? Well, it would appear that there is a place for both approaches. The top-down and bottom-up approaches each has areas that they could best address if there is a sober understanding of what can and cannot be achieved through whichever approach. For example, the government-led, top-down initiatives may be ill equipped at nurturing a startup culture at the grassroots, a feat better tackled by the hubs. However, if the hubs do a great job at nurturing a vibrant startup, innovation and entrepreneurship culture, it is inevitable that some of the startups that come out of these hubs will succeed, some of them may even go from 'garage-level' startup to multi-billion dollar enterprises much as we have seen with Facebook and others - at that time, the tech parks and cities will come in handy to provide the special 'economic zones', with the right infrastructure and environment for an enterprise operating at that scale.

Learning from 'the Valley'

Replicating Silicon Valley may not be entirely possible. For one, it is impossible to replicate the exact sequence of events and factors that came in to contribute to creating the unique culture that has developed in that area. However, we can learn a lot from what has worked and what hasn't, and we can even improve on that further to create an even more effective and efficient model, and even create such an environment in a much shorter period.

So what can we learn from Silicon Valley?

One of the contemporary luminaries of Silicon Valley is Paul Graham, the founder of the widely successful Y-Combinator, a startup accelerator that provides seed money, advice and industry connections to startups. Paul is also known for his insightful essays on startups and entrepreneurship. In 2006, he wrote a relevant essay to this topic "*How to be Silicon Valley*" (see references). Drawing from his essay, here's what Silicon Valley is and is not:

What Silicon Valley is Not - According to Graham, the Silicon Valley culture is not about buildings i.e. building a fancy technology park will not in itself lead to the springing up of a vibrant local startup culture. It may get you multinationals but it may not get you local innovation at scale.

What Silicon Valley is - According to Graham, the Valley is actually more about getting the right people than anything else. The right kind of smart, creative, innovative people who are motivated to start companies; and the right kind of people with the resources to invest in those companies.

In other words, Silicon Valley is less about the "*hard matter*" than it is about the "*soft matter*". It's hard to make an argument of there being absolutely no contribution of the "hard matter", to the making of Silicon Valley; after all, the universities which breed the smart nerds who create the cool products and services that Valley companies are built around have to have the right infrastructure and built in the right places, for example. But it is definitely clear that the "soft matter" is the key ingredient.

Ironically, the US government had a major hand in seeding the vibrant, innovative startup culture at Silicon Valley, albeit indirectly, through it's military spending during the Second World War. So don't make the proverbial mistake of 'throwing out the baby with the bathwater' by tossing out the top-down efforts of governments altogether.

In the "*Secret History of Silicon Valley*", Steve Blank traces back the history of the Valley beyond what is common knowledge to the real roots of the Valley. His exposition, takes us back to the early 40s and the Second World War, and how the early fathers of the Valley were actually professors who were funded by the state to come up with innovative ways to advance the American pursuit of success against the Germans.

Silicon Valley, A Habitat for Innovation and Entrepreneurship

What Silicon Valley is, and what the different efforts - whether top-down or bottom-up - are trying to achieve in Africa really, is the creation of a habitat - a supportive environment in which innovation and startups will be conceived, be nurtured and grow into full-blown, massively successful companies.

A 'habitat' comprises certain factors that create an environment suitable for the growth and flourishing of whatever it is that exists within it - for example, it is evident that some flora and fauna need tropical habitats, others need maritime habitats and so on, which comprise the right altitude, temperatures, quantity of rainfall, humidity and so on. So what comprises the kind of habitat that we see in the Valley and that are trying to be developed by governments and other entities?

In 2000, Stanford University Press published a book that answers exactly this question by looking at the Silicon Valley Habitat. In "*The Silicon Valley Edge: A Habitat for Innovation and Entrepreneurship*", various authors analyze ten specific elements that contribute to the "Valley Habitat." These should be the desirable outcomes of the efforts of public and private sector initiatives that are aiming at creating startup ecosystem in different parts of Africa:

1. Favorable rules of the game: laws, regulations, and conventions for securities, taxes, accounting, corporate governance, bankruptcy, immigration, research and development, and more.

2. Knowledge intensity: There is an amazing capacity within the Valley for the creation, assimilation and sharing of both technical and non-technical knowledge about products, services, markets, and business models.

3. A high quality and mobile workforce: The Valley concentrates a set of amazing talent within geography. Universities play a key role in providing the right kind of education, and more importantly exposure to the industry. Highly skilled individuals are rapidly assimilated into companies in the Valley where they are put to demanding tasks that push them to be creative and go the extra mile. Furthermore, this workforce is highly mobile. The demand for talent is very high, with major players jostling to get the best and the brightest.

4. Results-oriented meritocracy: "In the Valley, talent and ability are king". The habitat affords for identifying, nurturing and rewarding talent. You get ahead by what you know and how good you are at what you do.

5. A climate that rewards risk-taking and tolerates failure: Failure is not frowned upon in the Valley; on the contrary, it is seen as a way of learning. Many entrepreneurs have experienced failure at their first startup(s), but the environment makes it easy for them to draw their lessons from that experience and move on to a new idea and a new startup. This is one of the most unique aspects about the Silicon Valley habitat. In many African cultures, failure is not tolerated. When you're down you're considered to be out. This is clearly going to have to change. Favorable rules of the game also allow individuals to be bold about taking the risk to start companies and make bold initiatives.

6. Open business environment: Sharing is at the core of the Valley habitat. Knowledge that is not company secret is freely shared and others can adopt, adapt and apply shared knowledge in other ways. One example of this is how tech firms release some of their code as Open Source.

7. Universities and research institutes that interact with industry: The classic example here is Stanford University and its close tie to the Valley. The culture of allowing faculty to engage in industry as consultants and board members goes back decades (see references "*The Secret History of Silicon Valley*"). Companies also make contributions back to the universities by funding research and other such initiatives. This is another key piece that is largely missing in many African settings where in many cases there's a huge gap between industry and academia.

8. Collaborations among business, government, and nonprofit organizations: Collaboration in the Valley goes beyond just companies and universities. Everyone is welcome to play as long as they are advancing the Valley and stick to Valley culture.

9. High quality life: The Bay Area makes for a good environment. Mbwana emphasizes the importance of having a good work-life balance in (see the chapter, "*Which*

African country is best to do a tech startup? A Decision Framework")

10. Specialized business infrastructure: venture capitalists and bankers, lawyers, headhunters, accountants, consultants etc who are baked into the Valley culture.

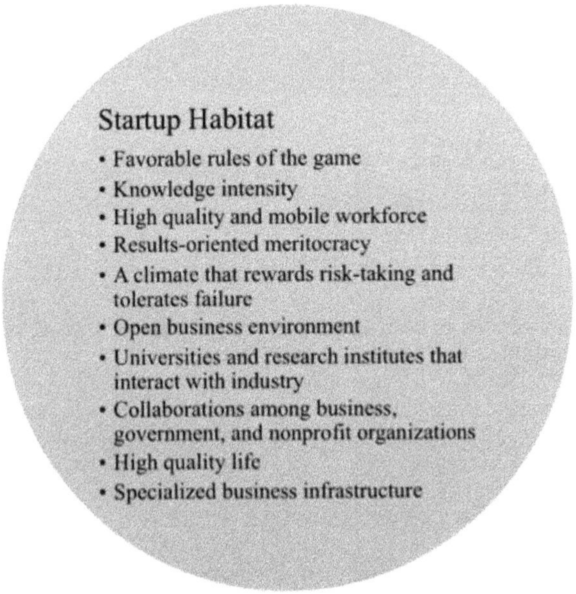

Startup Habitat
- Favorable rules of the game
- Knowledge intensity
- High quality and mobile workforce
- Results-oriented meritocracy
- A climate that rewards risk-taking and tolerates failure
- Open business environment
- Universities and research institutes that interact with industry
- Collaborations among business, government, and nonprofit organizations
- High quality life
- Specialized business infrastructure

Figure 13: The Startup Habitat

Conclusion

It is evident that at the end of the day, what matters is to create the right habitat and innovation and entrepreneurship will flourish. This is what matters and this is what should be the central premise to whatever initiative - government or private sector, top-down or bottom-up, technology park or hub.

References:

The Silicon Valley Edge, Edited by Chong-Moon Lee, William F. Miller, Marguerite Gong Hancock, and Henry S. Rowen, Stanford University Press, http://www.sup.org/ancillary.cgi?isbn=0804740631&item=Overview.htm

The Secret History of Silicon Valley, Steve Blank, http://steveblank.com/secret-history/

Next Silicon Valley, Riding the Waves of Innovation, The Next Silicon Valley Leadership Group, December 2001, http://www.coecon.com/publications/Waves_of_Innovation.pdf

Lessons from Silicon Valley and the Bay Area, Hartmut Siemon,

http://www.bridges.de/Download/OECD%20Silicon%20Valley.pdf

Mining the Silicon Valley Mind – A Perspective, Carlos Baradello, June 29, 2012,

http://carlosbaradello.com/2012/06/29/mining-the-silicon-valley-mind-a-perspective/

How to Be Silicon Valley, Paul Graham, May 2006,

http://www.paulgraham.com/siliconvalley.html

http://www.paulgraham.com/siliconvalley.html, Caroline Simard and Joel West, October 2005,

http://openinnovation.berkeley.edu/ranp_chapters/11.pdf

Entrepreneurship Models of the Countries that Leverage Silicon Valley, Mustafa Ergen, Fall 2004,

http://wow.eecs.berkeley.edu/ergen/docs/mainIAS.pdf

The Rise of Startup Ecosystems: Silicon Valley vs. New York vs. London, Rip Empson, April 2012,

http://techcrunch.com/2012/04/10/startup-genome-compares-top-startup-hubs/

How To Be A Silicon Valley Lawyer: A Tribute To Craig Johnson, by Scott Edward Walker on December 15th, 2010, http://walkercorporatelaw.com/lawyers/how-to-be-a-silicon-valley-lawyer-a-tribute-to-craig-johnson/

Listing the African Tech Hubs, oAfrica, April 2011, http://www.oafrica.com/business/african-tech-hubs/

Konza City: Does Kenya Really Need It?, Martin Carstens, March 2012, http://memeburn.com/2012/03/konza-technology-city-does-kenya-really-need-it/

Kenya: For Start-Ups, Tech Hub Anytime, Not Konza City, Kahenya Kamunyu, February 2012, http://allafrica.com/stories/201202270142.html

Public-private agreement set to establish ICT park, The Citizen, April 2011, http://thecitizen.co.tz/news/4-national-news/10099-public-private-agreement-set-to-establish-ict-park.html

Nigeria to launch largest science and technology park in Africa, AfricaBrains, http://africanbrains.net/2011/02/23/nigeria-to-launch-largest-science-and-technology-park-in-africa/

Nigeria: Lagos, CBC Partner On Technology Park Development, Efem Nkanga, AllAfrica, March 2011, http://allafrica.com/stories/201103100692.html

Ghana to build its first technology park, Galgallo Duba Fayo, HumanIPO, May 2012, http://www.humanipo.com/blog/347/Ghana-to-build-its-first-technology-park

Egypt's Smart Village Wants to be Regional IT Hub, Balancing Act Africa, Issue #186, http://www.balancingact-africa.com/news/en/issue-no-186/computing/egypt-s-smart-villag/en

Looking East: Observations and Lessons for Africa from China's Startup Ecosystem and Special Economic Zones

By Will Mutua

Many times when discussing the development of innovative technology ecosystems in Africa, we tend to look to the West and what we can learn from the likes of Silicon Valley (see the chapter *"The Making of Silicon Valleys in Africa"*). But could it be that we can learn and benefit from the East as well? It stands to reason that Africa and Africans indeed can, and in fact should study and engage both Eastern and Western models, to come up with homegrown hybrid models to the development of knowledge economies and innovative high tech sectors. To be sure, China is not the only Asian power that Africa can draw inspiration and "how-tos" from, not only in the technology sector but also in overall economic development models. Several countries are borrowing lessons from the likes of Singapore and Malaysia. China, however, is a practical heavyweight in Africa that has risen to challenge traditional Western collaborators and even donor organizations.

China has had a long history in Africa, though their engagement in the continent has only stepped into high gear in the recent past.

Back-story: China's economic engagement in Africa

China's recent activities in Africa have drawn mixed reactions from many quarters; some hold it to be a largely positive thing whilst there are those who would label China neo-colonialist and only seeking to take advantage of Africa's vast natural resources. For sure, China has a great interest in Africa and her natural resources – oil and minerals.

A quick look at the statistics is telling of China's interest in Africa: In 1980, the total Sino-African trade volume was US$1 billion. In 1999, it was US$6.5 billion and in 2000, US$10 billion. By 2005, the total Sino-African trade had reached US$39.7 billion before it jumped to US$55 billion in 2006, making China the second largest trading partner of Africa after the United States, which had trade worth US$91 billion with African nations. In 2010, trade between Africa and China was worth US$114 billion and 2011 saw a 33% increase to $166 billion comprising Chinese imports from Africa of about US $93 billion, (mostly mineral ores, petroleum, and agricultural products) and Chinese exports to Africa totaling $93 billion, comprising largely of manufactured goods. In the first five months of 2012, imports from Africa were up 25.5% to $49.6 billion while exports of Chinese-made products, increased 17.5% to reach $30.9 billion.

The intricacies of the Sino-African relationship are best left outside the scope of our consideration but one thing is for sure – the Chinese are serious about their engagement in Africa and they are here for the long haul.

In previous chapters we have looked at the contrast in approaches being taken by governments and private sectors to creating vibrant, innovative, entrepreneurial, tech-based, knowledge based economies (See *The Making of Silicon Valleys in Africa*").

We described the "Top-Down" approach being pursued primarily by government, that involves the creation of technology parks and cities; we also looked at the primarily private sector backed "Bottom Up" initiatives that are embodied in tech and innovation hubs. We can draw lessons from China that with regards to both strategies: China's *Special Economic Zones* (SEZs) have been instrumental in shaping her economy and really turning up

China's economic engines to high gear. The same method has been applied to foster industrial and economic progress in other Asian countries, with particular applications in the East Asian economies. On the other hand, China has a unique startup ecosystem that is backed by traditional VC and private equity. Indeed, China's startup scene is very different from the Silicon Valley startup scene; we can also draw on this to glean some lessons that could apply to fostering startup ecosystems around Africa.

Let's first turn our attention to the Chinese startup scene, one that is pretty unique as compared to the standard model for startup ecosystems- Silicon Valley:

China's Startup Ecosystem

The Chinese startup ecosystem has been described as challenging, messy and different. China's startup center is Zhongguancun. The hub boasts a strong academic center with China's top two universities, Peking and Tsinghua University, alongside a host of technical universities located in the area, as well as research centers and large technology firms.

China's tech scene is dominated by a handful of large players including *Tencent* which boasts China's premier internet portal and focuses on gaming and instant messaging services, e-commerce giant *Alibaba*, search engine *Baidu,* and *Qihoo 360*, an internet and mobile security products company. Other notable companies that have built a strong following are: *RenRen*, a social networking site built along the lines of Facebook, *WeiBo*, a micro-blogging service along the lines of Twitter, *DianPing*, the 'China's *Yelp*', *Kaixin*, a social gaming company and the recently merged *ToDou* and *YouKu* which offer a YouTube-like online video sharing service. The fact that China's Internet world is closed off from the rest of the world to a large extent means that local companies can emulate successes outside China to target the local market with a pretty high degree of success. And with over 500 million Internet users (less than 250M in the US), as well as over a billion mobile users (as compared to just over 300M in the US), there exists a huge online market.

According to data from a presentation by Taylor Cox of the Zhen Fund, a startup investment fund in China (see references), there were 1,500 VC deals worth $13 billion in China in 2011with about 268 of those deals being in Internet companies, representing $3.2 billion in funding. Telecommunications, Media and Technology (TMT) are also booming in China. According to 2012 H1 data from

Zero2IPO Research covering the Venture Capital and Private Equity (VC/PE) market in China, 401 VC deals were made. 322 of those disclosed a total of US $2.5B. To break this down to relevant sectors-

- Internet: 72 deals amounting to US $470.90M,

- IT: 39 deals amounting to US $217.06M,

- Telecom & value-added services: 31 deals amounting to US $237.73M.

On the PE front: 252 investment deals were closed, with 218 disclosing a combined US $7.32B in investment. Breaking it down again to relevant sectors:

- Internet: 21 deals and US $ 174M,

- IT: 8 deals and US $17M

- Telecoms & value added services: 11 deals and US $283M in investment.

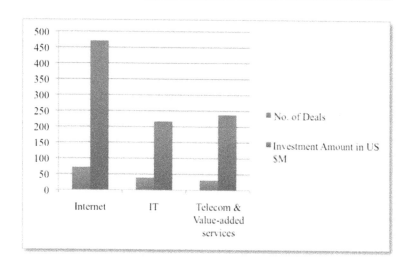

Figure 14: VC deals in China by sector. Data source: Zero2IPO China VC/PE Market Review H1 2012

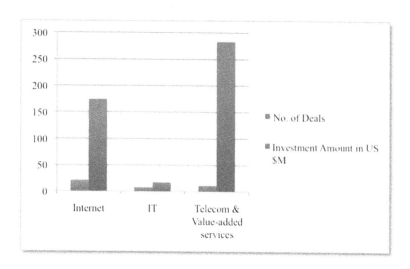

Figure 15: PE deals in China by sector. Data source: Zero2IPO China VC/PE Market Review H1 2012

Drawing Lessons from the Chinese Startup Ecosystem

Interestingly, there are several characteristics of the Chinese startup and innovation culture and ecosystem that can be compared and contrasted with what's happening in Africa and that we can learn from.

Note that the aim here is to look at broad similarities and broad differences, the vast difference in scale (number of startups, number of listed companies, size of companies, size of VC/PE markets) and the fact that China is a single entity while Africa consists of many countries with different regimes and cultures definitely makes it impossible to draw straight lines between the Chinese startup scene and Africa.

The Similarities

Cool apps don't cut it in China: Kai Lukoff, the founder of TechRice – an English language tech blog that covers the Chinese tech scene, notes that in China, building cool apps for iOS is not a sure fire way of being a successful startup. In Africa, the same applies; if you want to build a big tech company, cool apps are not the easiest path to follow. Feature phones still dominate the market, though the introduction of cheaper, low-end, Android-based Smartphones is set to change that. *Utility beats coolness in Africa.* Using ubiquitous technologies such as USSD and SMS are sure ways to get adoption at scale.

The risk of being copied: In China, copycats abound. For example, by some estimates there are over 3000 Groupon clones in China. Just about every cool thing that comes along from Silicon Valley spawns multiple clones in China. For some reason, the culture tends towards viewing trying to replicate something that's worked somewhere else as less risky. It's also evident that the big players will usually not acquire small startups that are doing something interesting but instead copy what they are doing and offer the same service to their massive user bases. In fact, mergers and acquisitions are not as prevalent as IPO exits in China. In (at least some parts of) Africa, budding entrepreneurs in tech usually have to be cautious of their idea being taken by some larger entity, which has led to some treading very carefully and not sharing their ideas and initiatives openly.

Cultural conservatism: Culturally, the Chinese are not as risk and failure-tolerant as the US counterparts. This is something we see in many African cultures where the security of employment is sometimes preferred to the uncertainty of entrepreneurship. Perhaps this explains the prevalence of copy-and-paste business strategies in China as we have previously seen. It can be argued that this kind of culture develops as a kind of self-defense mechanism against the realities of unemployment and poverty.

Not as open as the US: The startup culture in China is not as open as it is in Silicon Valley. There isn't much sharing in terms of, for example, sharing source code so that others can adapt, remix and use proven technology. The same applies in many parts of Africa. Many young entrepreneurs in Africa are not willing to share ideas and many go to great lengths to protect those ideas with a perceived or real risk of their idea being copied by a better resourced person or company that then goes ahead and implements it. It is common practice to have parties sign Non-Disclosure Agreements before proceeding to discuss things even at the idea stage. This kind of culture is foreign in Silicon Valley, where the mentality is that ideas are a dime a dozen and if you've thought about it someone else already has.

Lack of serial entrepreneurs and successful entrepreneurs-turned-investors: In the Chinese ecosystem, as in Africa's, there are relatively fewer successful entrepreneurs that turn back and become investors in startups themselves. Africa, generally, is farther behind, and the situation in South Africa is different from that in Kenya, or Ghana or Senegal. The likes of Alibaba, Baidu and the big players of the Chinese Internet startup scene are likely to churn out potential investors and perhaps the likes of the so-called PayPal Mafia in Silicon Valley. In places like Kenya, local investors are still more secure with their investments in other areas such as real estate. Also, the fact that there are few technology entrepreneurs turned investors means that startups are getting little technical value add, in addition to money.

Difficulty setting up a company: It is notoriously difficult to set up a company in China, particularly for foreign companies. According to the World Bank Ease of Doing Business Index, China ranks 91 overall and 151 in terms of ease of starting a business. The same can be said of some African countries where the ease of doing business is terrible. The sheer amount of time, cost and procedural burden to register a business in some cases crushes out the entrepreneurial spirit, not to mention the risk of corruption. Furthermore, government policies can have an adverse effect on free enterprise.

The Differences

Hardware companies not so prevalent in Africa: Innovation in hardware is still in its infancy in Africa. There have been several attempts at creating local hardware companies such as the Congolese tablet computer manufacturer VMK started by Verone Mankou and others. In China however, hardware companies are pervasive. The *Shanzhai*, are renown for coming up with knock-off mobile phones, many of which have found their way to African markets. Several tech and innovation hubs across Africa are taking initiatives to promote innovation in hardware.

Funding for tech startups is still a challenge in Africa: The VC/PE market in China is generally huge and there's much more funding available for technology companies as compared to Africa. For example, according to the joint South Africa Venture Capital Association (SAVCA) and KPMG... the reported value of private equity investments amounted to R15.6 billion (approx. US $1.86 billion) during 2011 (up 32.2% from a figure of Rand 11.8 billion or approx. US $1.4 billion), the top three investment sectors being infrastructure - 31.9% of investments, 6.4% in the retail sector and 6.4% in the manufacturing sector. Private Equity investment in Information Technology actually went down from 0.8% in 2010, telecoms accounted for 3.2% (up from 1.7%)

Exits: IPOs (Initial Public Offers) and M&A (Mergers and Acquisitions) are not yet prevalent for technology startups in Africa. There are few cases of technology companies that have gone from startup phase to IPO or have merged / been acquired by larger companies. The markets are developing, though, and some have shown brilliant performance such as the Nairobi Stock Exchange (NSE) that was ranked the third best performing stock exchange (see references). The NSE has also been planning a specialized market segment targeted at Small and Medium Enterprises (SMEs); this could perhaps bring the possibility of listing publicly closer to reality for technology startups.

Brain drain: We have previously considered Africa's brain drain challenge (see chapter *"Research and Development in Sub-Saharan Africa: The Current Situation"*). China, on the other hand, has been very successful at drawing back the so-called *haigui* or "sea turtles", Chinese students and professionals who are returning home from abroad. The skilled and experienced managers and engineers are coming back in tens and hundreds of thousands and finding their place within the Chinese economy. By one estimate

135,000 haigui re-entered China in 2010 according to an article on the Global Post titled, *"How China's "sea turtles" will crush the US economy"* (see references).

Special Economic Zones (SEZs)

China's first SEZs were set up in the 1980s as a channel for drawing in Foreign Direct Investment by creating specialized areas that foster economic growth. They act as centers to draw in private sector investment while at the same time allowing the government to channel specific economic policies to a limited area; these policies could include tax incentives. Three decades since the earliest SEZs in China were set up in the in Shenzhen, Zhuhai, Shantou and Xiamen, the model has proven itself. Today, there are over a hundred SEZs and industrial clusters in China. In those three decades, China has perfected the art of using Special Economic Zones to spur the economy.

Even more interesting, is that China is in the process of transferring the same model to Africa by setting up SEZs in different African countries. Although the six SEZs that are currently underway in Africa are not technology focused, African governments can learn the model and perhaps apply it to technology-based industries.

Location	Industry
Chambishi, Zambia	Copper and copper related industries
Lusaka, Zambia	Garments, food, appliances, tobacco and electronics. This zone is classified as a subzone of the Chambishi zone
Jinfei, Mauritius	Manufacturing (textiles, garments, machinery, high-tech), trade, tourism and finance.
Oriental, Ethiopia	Electrical machinery, construction materials, steel and metallurgy
Ogun, Nigeria	Construction materials, ceramics, ironware, furniture, wood processing, medicine, and computers.
Lekki, Nigeria	Transportation equipment, textiles, home appliances, telecommunications, and light industry
Suez, Egypt	Petroleum equipment, electrical appliance, textile and automobile manufacturers

Table 5: China's Special Economic Zones in Africa

The technology parks that we discussed in a previous chapter (See "*The Making of Silicon Valleys in Africa*") follow more or less the same 'top-down' principles – creating focused localities for concentration of technological industry.

The key to the success of this model is strong commitment, strong leadership and the active, pragmatic facilitation of the state to make it work.

Conclusion and Lessons

While, as we have noted, China's technology scene is at a different scale as compared to Africa's, there are indeed similarities that can form a basis to draw lessons from, as Africa tries to grow her technology and innovation ecosystem:

1. Low appetite for risk and intolerance to failure stifle innovation: This leads to people being over-protective of ideas and prevents openness and sharing. It can also mean that people will turn to copy-and-paste strategies that are anti-innovation

2. There needs to be an open environment where people are not threatened of each other. For example, sharing code means that smaller

companies can stand on the shoulders of giants, in a manner of speaking. While the 2-person upstart may not have the engineering capacity to create something from scratch, they can borrow from open-source libraries published by companies that have hundreds of engineers.

3. Pursuing multiple strategies is a good thing: A mix of top-down and bottom-up initiatives will get us there

4. Top-down initiatives can succeed in the long term but need strong leadership and commitment, especially from the government.

5. Efficient funding mechanisms are crucial. In addition, extra value-add to monetary support is necessary. Mentorship, both in terms of how to run a business as well as more technical handholding is particularly important.

6. Reversing brain drain: It is crucial that Africa and Africa's nations figure out how to draw back or tap into those skilled and experienced Africans who are studying and working abroad.

References:

China in Africa:

The Dragon's Gift: The Real Story of China in Africa, Deborah Brautigam, http://www.amazon.com/The-Dragons-Gift-Story-Africa/dp/0199550220

Winner Take All, Dambisa Moyo, http://www.dambisamoyo.com/books-and-publications/book/winner-take-all

Africa-China Relations, Wikipedia, http://en.wikipedia.org/wiki/China_in_Africa

Africa-China Economic Relations, Wikipedia, http://en.wikipedia.org/wiki/Africa%E2%80%93China_economic_relations

Beijing, a Boon for Africa, Dambisa Moyo, The New York Times, June 2012, http://www.nytimes.com/2012/06/28/opinion/beijing-a-boon-for-africa.html

China's Startup Ecosystem

The China Startup Report, Bowei Gai, October 2011, http://www.slideshare.net/bowei/the-china-startup-report-a-15min-crash-course-by-bowei-gai

China's Entrepreneurship Ecosystem, ZhenFund, 2012,
http://www.slideshare.net/ZhenFund/chinas-startup-ecosystem

Bringing your start-up to the Chinese market, Chris Evedmon, September 2009,
http://www.slideshare.net/evdemon/startup-in-china

China VC/PE Market Review H1 2012, Gavin Ni, Zero2IPO Group, July 2012,
http://www.zero2ipo.com.cn/promotion/survey/2011/China%20VCPE%20Market%20Review%202011_EN.pdf

Technology Start-up Scenario and VC, PE funding (India vs. China), Amit Goel & Yagna Teja, February 2012,
http://www.slideshare.net/yagnateja/technology-start-up-scenario-and-vcpe-funding-india-vs-china

A Geek's Guide to China's Silicon Valley, Kai Lukoff, December 2011, http://techcrunch.com/2011/12/27/geeks-guide-china-silicon-valley/

Zhongguancun, China's Silicon Valley,
http://www.china.org.cn/english/travel/51023.htm

The startup guide to China, Jon Russel, The Next Web, August 2012,

http://thenextweb.com/asia/2012/08/12/startup-guide-china

China's Special Economic Zones

The potential of Special Economic Zones (SEZs) in Africa, Rafeeat Aliyu,

http://www.consultancyafrica.com/index.php?option=com_
content&view=article&id=806:the-potential-of-special-
economic-zones-sezs-in-africa&catid=58:asia-dimension-
discussion-papers&Itemid=264

China's Special Economic Zones and Industrial Clusters: Success and Challenges, Douglas Zhihua Zeng,

http://blogs.worldbank.org/developmenttalk/node/618

China's Special Economic Zones in Africa, Deborah Brautigam,

http://www.chinaafricarealstory.com/2011/02/chinas-
special-economic-zones-in-africa.html

Africa: WEF Africa 2012 - Africa's Special Economic Zones, Eleanor Whitehead & Adam Robert Green,

http://allafrica.com/stories/201205291262.html

China's Investment in African Special Economic Zones: Prospects, Challenges, and Opportunities, Deborah Brautigam, Economic Premise, March 2010, http://www.scribd.com/doc/30513841/China%E2%80%99s -Investment-in-African-Special-Economic-Zones- Prospects-Challenges-and-Opportunities-Deborah- Brautigam-Thomas-Farole-and-Tang-Xiaoyan

Others

Ease of Doing Business in China, http://www.doingbusiness.org/data/exploreeconomies/china /

KPMG and SAVCA Venture Capital and Private Equity Industry Performance Survey of South Africa covering the 2011 calendar year, May 2012, http://www.kpmg.com/ZA/en/IssuesAndInsights/ArticlesPu blications/General-Industries- Publications/Documents/Private%20Equity%20survey%20 2012.pdf

How China's "sea turtles" will crush the US economy, Benjamin Carlson, Global Post, http://www.globalpost.com/dispatch/news/regions/asia-pacific/china/120717/sea-turtles-haigui-overseas-educated-return-home

'Sea turtles' reverse China's brain drain, Jaime FlorCruz, CNN, http://articles.cnn.com/2010-10-28/world/florcruz.china.sea.turtles.overseas_1_china-chinese-experts-overseas-chinese-students?_s=PM:WORLD

Kenya Stocks Lure Templeton to World's Third-Best Rally, Erik Ombok, Bloomberg News, http://www.businessweek.com/news/2012-06-27/kenya-stocks-lure-templeton-to-world-s-third-biggest-rally

Kenya stock exchange to start SME segment by 2012, Reuters Africa, http://af.reuters.com/article/kenyaNews/idAFL5E7JO1PS20110824

Necessity & Invention: Africa's story of mobile conquest & why utility beats 'coolness', Will Mutua, http://afrinnovator.com/blog/2011/11/18/necessity-invention-africas-story-of-mobile-conquest-why-utility-beats-coolness/

China Web Video Sites Youku, Tudou Agree To Merge, Eric Savitz, http://www.forbes.com/sites/ericsavitz/2012/03/12/china-web-video-sites-youku-tudou-agree-to-merge/

From Startup Clusters to Startup Nations
By Will Mutua

In the last chapter, we looked at China's startup culture and ecosystem, drawing a few broad lessons from it. One key note that makes it difficult to draw straight lines between China and Africa is that while 'Africa' is used as a blanket term, the reality on the ground holds that it is not a homogenous, singular, national entity, but actually more than 50 different countries, thousands of languages and dialects, multiple cultures and sub-cultures, different political and governmental regimes, different economic profiles, and even drastically different colonial experiences. Even at the regional level, there are significant differences between regions; Francophone Africa is a world of a difference from Anglophone Africa. China, on the other hand, presents a more unified picture that is easier to read. In addition, the populations of China and the African continent as a whole may be fairly similar – roughly a billion strong each – but when you drill down to country level you have on one extreme, Nigeria with a population of over 160 million and on the other extreme you have Equatorial Guinea with just over 700,000 people (not to mention islands that have numbers in the thousands)! Economically, Africa has been billed as a resource rich continent as a whole, and while that may be true, the actual distribution of natural resources is not uniform throughout the continent.

This is why African nations could learn a thing or two from a 64-year old nation with a population of about 7.8 million that has no natural resources to boast of, scarcity of arable land and water sources, that has been ravaged by war after war since independence, yet has the third highest number of companies listed on the NASDAQ exchange (after the US and China), an extremely high concentration of startups and VC per capita. This is the same nation that spawned *Snaptu*, a mobile service that was later acquired by Facebook very recently. It is also the nation that brought us the first Instant Messaging service, ICQ (later acquired by AOL), innovations in Intel's chips that resulted in the creation of the Centrino chip for laptops as well as revolutionizing the microprocessor industry, and many more inventions, innovations and discoveries.

In addition, multiple multinational technology companies including Intel, Microsoft, Google, Cisco and Motorola maintain critical operations in this country, particularly for their Research and Development units.

That nation is **Israel**.

Israel has come to be known as the '*Startup Nation*'. In a 2009 book, by Saul Singer and Dan Senor by the same title, the authors explore the mystery of Israel's amazing innovation and entrepreneurship capacity.

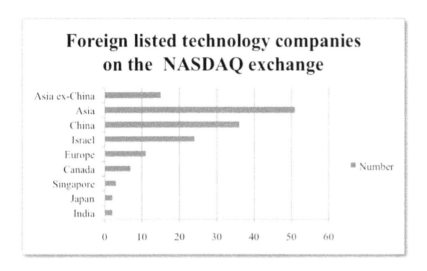

Figure 16: Number of foreign technology companies on NASDAQ

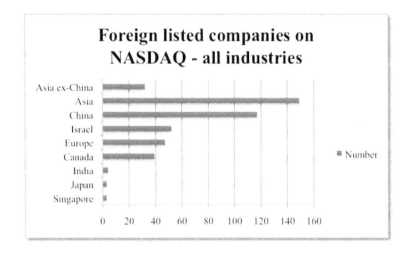

Figure 17: Number of foreign companies on NASDAQ

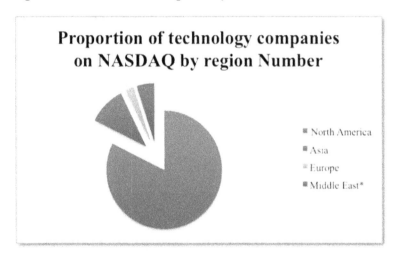

Figure 18: Proportion of technology companies on NASDAQ by region

*All the foreign NASDAQ listed companies from the Middle East are Israeli

According to a survey by the Israel Venture Capital (IVC) Research Center and KPMG Somekh Chaikin, Israeli start ups raised $2.14 billion in 2011, the highest amount raised in the last 11 years, 70% more than the $1.26 billion raised in 2010, and 91% more than the $1.12 billion raised in 2009. The latest figures published by IVC-KPMG indicate that Israeli venture capital investments in the first half of 2012 reached $936 million, a decrease of 11 percent from $1.05 billion invested in the first half of 2011, but 62 percent above the $577 million invested in the corresponding 2010 period.

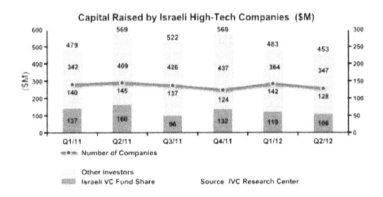

Figure 19: Capital raised by Israeli high-tech companies

Israel also boasts the highest number of startup companies in proportion to her population and is second only to the US in absolute terms.

What observations can we draw from Israel and can we learn from the 'Startup Nation'?

It's important to note once more that the attempt here is not to draw direct comparison. The aim is to glean general lessons and principles that can be used as insight for developing homegrown innovation and entrepreneurial ecosystems in individual countries within their own context.

Starting Early

In their book, Dan Senor and Saul Singer make the argument that the Israeli Defense Forces (IDF) has been crucial to shaping the entrepreneurial and innovative nature of Israel's citizens. In Israel, it is mandatory for most young Israelis to undertake up to three years of military service (2 years for women and 3 for men) before transitioning to university (typically between 19 and 21 years of age). The IDF experience, the authors argue, gives these young people an experience that is difficult to find anywhere else in the world for such an age group. The military imparts discipline, leadership skills, teamwork, problem solving, mission orientation and other critical life skills such that by the time they are going into university they are at a completely different level in terms of maturity, perspective, and life experience. In addition, it instills a 'die-hard' mentality and so you find an unusual resilience in Israeli companies. As an example, the authors tell the story of *Iscar*, a company in which Warren Buffet invested ($4 billion for 80% of the company). Shortly after the Buffet's investment, Israel was caught up in the 2006 Lebanon war. Eitan Wertheimer, who was the chairman of Iscar and who had made the sale to Buffet, called him up on the first day of the war and vowed to proceed operations unabated, despite some of their factories being prime targets for missile attacks. Even with half the workforce, Iscar did not miss a single shipment. Mr. Wertheimers attitude can be summarized thus: "*Wrecked machines can be replaced...We're going to carry on and ensure all customers get their orders on time or even earlier*"

In addition, the authors argue that it's not just that these young people get military experience but it's more the nature of the IDF experience. The IDF encourages innovation and questioning of authorities and decisions by even junior officers. The structure of the IDF is a very flat one with a very small top-level, officer corp, which means decision making is left to lower levels, and this encourages improvisation and innovation to get things done.

> *"The social graph is very simple here. Everybody knows everybody." - Yossi Vardi, Israeli high-tech entrepreneur*

The real difference comes as a result of the way the Israelis have managed to translate military experience into the world of private enterprise; skills, experiences and more importantly the networks formed as a result of the 2-3 year military stint. Many Israelis later on form companies with people they met during their military experience and the strong network means that if you need funding or some other resource for your startup, you can usually find what you need within your military-experience network. For instance, Shvat Shaked founded cybersecurity firm Fraud Sciences with a former Army intelligence colleague; PayPal later bought out the company for $169 million.

The benefits are also translated in other ways such as the application of skills learnt in special units, particularly technological ones. Gavriel Iddan, a former rocket scientist who worked on sophisticated electro-optical, missile guiding devices, found a way to adapt the technology to the world of medicine and invented PillCams – miniature cameras in a small capsule that can be ingested and used to probe internal organs – and founded Given Imaging which later went public on Wall Street (the first company to do so post 9-11).

Lesson:

While Israel's situation, as far as perpetually being in a state of conflict and consequent heavy investments in maintaining a strong military is not desirable for any nation, the principal take-out here is the kind of experience that Israelis get at a fairly young age.

There are other ways of creating the same experience outside the military. These could be programs within universities, for example, or whatever else. The thing is that it's done at a national level so the culture created by the IDF, for example, is pervasive to the entire population, creating a 'Startup Nation'.

If you manage to shape the culture of a population into one that embraces entrepreneurship and innovation from the earliest opportunity, you have a culture that is set up to succeed.

Necessity is the mother of invention

Since independence, Israel has been in a constant state of conflict and war. This, as we have seen, has led of necessity to the creation of an exceptional military. Not only that, but Israel has a lot of other things that are not going for it: the climate, water shortage and the tiny nation basically has no natural resources to speak of. Yet, out of necessity, Israel has had to turn up her innovative engines to meet the immense geopolitical challenges that face her.

Lesson:

Many African nations face similar (not the same) challenges – some have been ravaged by war, droughts and famine over their post-independence history. The perception of Africa in general as a war-torn, politically unstable, continent is very common especially given the kind of foreign media attention given to the continent.

However, challenges are also opportunities for innovation. African nations, with the right leadership and commitment, can turn odds into opportunities through innovation.

Mobile money and particularly MPESA in Kenya is a good example of innovation that turns a challenge into an opportunity: Why is MPESA such a success? Simply put – it was a necessity and it met a common problem.

Pre-MPESA, people still had to do all the things that MPESA has enabled them to do. In Kenya, most of the working class is in urban areas, their parents likely live in rural areas. In the Kenyan culture, it is ordinary and even expected of one to take care of their parents and even their siblings once they have the means to do so. This mostly means sending money back home to ones parents for all sorts of things – their upkeep; your siblings school fees etc.

Pre-MPESA, people still had fairly ingenious ways of accomplishing this – from sending a relative home with the cash, to using bus services to send the cash, to mailing the cash sandwiched between carbon paper so someone handling the post does not see the money through the envelope and decide to pocket it. MPESA simply solved a very real need that almost every (at least adult) Kenyan was facing, they did it simply – all you needed was a phone of whatever kind, they did it efficiently – MPESA agents are everywhere! And they did it at a reasonable cost to the consumer. Kenyans bought into it hook, line and sinker and Safaricom now draws huge revenues from the product, not to mention sparking an entire industry.

Culture of tolerance to risk and failure, debating and questioning

We saw it when we took a look at the case of Silicon Valley and yet again when looking at the case of China's startup ecosystems – the cultural tolerance to risk and failure is a critical ingredient to creating a startup culture. Take a look at Israeli culture and you will find the same.

In addition, the authors of Startup Nation present a unique aspect of Israeli culture – *chutzpah*. Chutzpah is a culture of intense debating and questioning; according to Yiddish scholar Leo Rosten, it is *"gall, brazen nerve, effrontery, incredible 'guts,' presumption, plus arrogance such as no other word and no other language can do justice to."* This culture is pervasive – in homes, at all levels of the education system, in companies and research institutes.

Lesson:

Culture is a dicey affair – it's simply either there or it isn't! Culture is not quantifiable and so one cannot approach it in an algorithmic manner. Plus, changing embedded cultural traits is difficult and can take an entire generational shift.

Many African cultures tend to be risk-averse and intolerant to failure and in many cases questioning authority is not looked well upon. There is a balance to this though – risk taking needs to be calculated and authority should be respected. However, total aversion of risk and fear of failure will not lead to the creation of startup culture and entrepreneurial and innovative spirit in a nation – these necessarily embody elements of risk and potential failure and are achieved, in part, through questioning the status quo, ("Why are things the way they are?" "Why are things not a different way than they are?") Healthy debate, trial and error

One thing that could work to the favor of African nations is that majority of the population is young (youth bulge). In a globalized world where these young people are exposed to the Internet and Web, mobile phones and other technologies, Africa's youth are being influenced by outside forces, they are much more exposed than previous generations, they are not in close touch with colonial pasts and are more willing to embrace the world, try out new things. Rightly handled, that population could turn African nations into innovation and entrepreneurial cauldrons.

R&D: Beyond spending to assimilation

Israel spends huge percentage of her GDP on Research and Development. According to the Organization for Economic Co-operation Development (OECD) Science, Technology and Industry Scoreboard 2011 (see references): *"Israel has the highest R&D intensity, with gross domestic expenditure on R&D (GERD) in excess of 4% of gross domestic product (GDP). The OECD average stands at 2.3%"*

We've already looked at the state of R&D in Africa as we saw most African nations spend a paltry amount on R&D, and in some cases, the value of R&D is not appreciated. However, the real value of R&D in Israel goes beyond spending.

First of all, *chutzpah* is a key ingredient in Israel's R&D facilities just as it is in the startup world; these are not just research facilities but institutions that have a startup culture baked in. Secondly, R&D is translated into the real world, being used in companies and solving real world problems.

Lesson:

African nations should not only find ways to encourage and invest more in R&D, but also, and more importantly, create a startup culture within R&D institutes. The link between R&D and industry is the key to turning great research into usable, marketable innovations. (See the chapter *"Research and Development in Sub-Saharan Africa: The Current Situation"*)

Government knowing and playing its part

The Israeli government, for example, played a key role in creating and shaping the Venture Capital industry in Israel. However, the government was smart enough to identify the role it could play in kick-starting VC in Israel, focused and stuck to executing only that part and then got out of the way. Upon identifying the lack of VC problem, the Israeli government took a deliberate decision to intervene and create one (the Yozma program), provided the funding to do so, got partners on board, sparked it and got it going and got out of the way. The result – Israel has the highest VC per capita.

Lesson:

Government in many cases in African nations has been a stumbling block rather than a stepping-stone. Dictatorial regimes and corrupt governments have not helped the situation. Furthermore, policies that discourage free enterprise such as burdensome company registration processes discourage potential entrepreneurs even more.

In order to turn a nation into an innovative and entrepreneurial one, the government inevitably has to come to the table and play its part. The thing to note here is *that government should adopt the philosophy of enabling and regulating without directly controlling or dictating how things should run.* There's a role for government to play and governments should stick to their part strictly. Over-involvement of government can lead to slow and tediously bureaucratic processes that do little to spur innovation and entrepreneurship or even altogether discourage the same.

Conclusion: Startup Nation = Entrepreneurial Culture + Innovation Culture

In reality, what we find in Israel is the combinations of two things that are the key ingredients of a startup culture: a *strong innovation culture* and a *strong entrepreneurial culture*. You can't have one without the other and find a vibrant startup culture. Innovation without entrepreneurship is nothing more than R&D. Yet just being entrepreneurial does not necessarily mean innovation is present – for example, many African nations have strong entrepreneurial culture, but starting a business does not mean you're creating something innovative.

This is not only true of Israel but of other startup clusters. The unique thing about Israel is that it is not localized, but pervasive in the entire nation. Perhaps African nations can look to Israel's model and borrow a leaf or two to transform themselves into startup nations.

References:

Startup Nation: The Story of Israel's Economic Miracle, Dan Senor & Saul Singer,

http://www.startupnationbook.com/

How Did Israel Become "Start-Up Nation"?, Dwyer Gunn, April 2009,
http://www.freakonomics.com/2009/12/04/how-did-israel-become-start-up-nation/

Where Tech Keeps Booming, The Wall Street Journal Online, November 2009,
http://online.wsj.com/article/SB100014240527487047797045745538842718 02474.html

The Origins of Israel's Tech Miracle, Jeffrey Goldberg, The Atlantic, November 2009,
http://www.theatlantic.com/international/archive/2009/11/the-origins-of-israels-tech-miracle/29570/

Lessons from a Startup Nation, Murat Seker, July 2012,
http://blogs.worldbank.org/psd/node/13124

What's Next for the Startup Nation?, The Economist, January 2012, http://www.economist.com/node/21543151

Necessity & Invention: Africa's story of mobile conquest & why utility beats 'coolness', Will Mutua,
http://afrinnovator.com/blog/2011/11/18/necessity-invention-africas-story-of-mobile-conquest-why-utility-beats-coolness/

OECD Science, Technology and Industry Scoreboard 2011, http://www.oecd-ilibrary.org/sites/sti_scoreboard-2011-en/02/05/index.html?contentType=&itemId=/content/chapter/sti_scoreboard-2011-16-en&containerItemId=/content/serial/20725345&accessItemIds=/content/book/sti_scoreboard-2011-en&mimeType=text/html

R&D Spending, The Economist, http://www.economist.com/node/21531002

Israel Venture Capital (IVC) Research Center, http://www.ivc-online.com/

IVC and KPMG 2012 H1 Venture Capital Report, http://www.ivc-online.com/Portals/0/RC/Survey/IVC-Q2-12-Survey-PR-Eng-Final.pdf

Israeli start ups raised $2.14b in 2011, Globes, http://www.globes.co.il/serveen/globes/docview.asp?did=1000718497&fid=1725

Venture Capital in Israel, Wikipedia, http://en.wikipedia.org/wiki/Venture_capital_in_Israel

VC Policy: Yozma Program 15-Year Perspective, Gil Avnimelech, 2009, http://www2.druid.dk/conferences/viewpaper.php?id=5606 &cf=32

The Yozma Group, http://www.yozma.com/overview/

http://www.nasdaq.com/screening/company-list.aspx

Listing Foreign Firms on Nasdaq and NYSE: Impact of Venture Capital and Research Institute, Mustafa Seref Akin, Department of Economics, Fatih University, Istanbul, Turkey, 2011, http://www.scirp.org/fileOperation/downLoad.aspx?path=I B20110400002_92984188.pdf&type=journal

Buffett Buys Israel's Iscar: The Oracle is No Messiah, Michael Eisenberg, 2006, http://seekingalpha.com/article/10199-buffett-buys-israel-s-iscar-the-oracle-is-no-messiah

Warren Buffett Invested In ISCAR; ISCAR's Founder Is Investing In Peace, Caleb Melby, Forbes, July 2012, http://www.forbes.com/sites/calebmelby/2012/03/07/warre n-buffett-invested-in-iscar-iscars-founder-is-investing-in-peace/

About the Authors

Will Mutua is the founder of Afrinnovator (http://afrinnovator.com), a knowledge organization that carries out research and consultancy on matters to do with technology, innovation and startups in Africa. Will is a keen observer of the African technology space and has a passion for technology and its transformative potential for Africa. He has a strong background in software engineering.

Mbwana Alliy is the founder and managing partner of Savannah Fund (http://www.savannah.vc/), an Africa focused, technology Venture Capital fund. He is passionate about product development and launching new ventures in technology. He is an experienced Product Manager within consumer web, enterprise Software & Software as a Service (SaaS) sectors. He is originally from Tanzania and has lived and worked in 3 continents (USA, Europe and Africa). He has a Bachelor's degree in engineering from Bristol University and an MBA from Stanford Graduate school of Business. Find out more about Mbwana at http://www.mbwana.com/bio.html

About Afrinnovator.com

Afrinnovator (http://afrinnovator.com) is a leading source of knowledge and information on technology, innovation and startups in Africa. Afrinnovator has gained global recognition and has established itself as an authority on matters regarding tech in Africa with a specific focus in Sub-Saharan Africa.

Follow Afrinnovator on Twitter (http://twitter.com/afrinnovator) for more. Contact Afrinnovator at info@afrinnovator.com